Dumfries *and* Galloway

W A L K S

Compiled by
Brian Conduit

JARROLD

Ordnance
Survey

Acknowledgements

The author is grateful for the invaluable advice and assistance that he received from Dumfries and Galloway Regional Council and the various tourist information offices throughout the area.

Text: Brian Conduit
Photography: Brian Conduit
Editor: Julie Beesley, Donald Greig
Designers: Brian Skinner, Doug Whitworth
Mapping: Heather Pearson, Sandy Sims

Series Consultant: Brian Conduit

Jarrold Publishing   ISBN 0-7117-0671-9

First published 1997
by Jarrold Publishing and Ordnance Survey

Printed in Great Britain
by Jarrold Book Printing, Thetford, Norfolk 1/97

Jarrold Publishing,
Whitefriars, Norwich NR3 1TR
Ordnance Survey,
Romsey Road, Southampton SO16 4GU

Front cover: Carlingwark Loch, Castle Douglas
Previous page: Caerlaverock Castle

Contents

The Law and Tradition as they affect Walking in Scotland; Scotland's Hills and Mountains: a Concordat on Access; Glossary of Gaelic names;Safety on the Hills; Useful Organisations; Ordnance Survey Maps

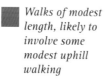

■ Short, easy walks

■ Walks of modest length, likely to involve some modest uphill walking

■ More challenging walks which may be longer and/or over more rugged terrain, often with some stiff climbs

Keymap 1

SCALE 1:312 500 or 1 INCH to 5 MILES *1CM to 3.1 KM*

0 2 4 6 8 10 KILOMETRES 15

0 2 4 6 MILES 8 10

KEYMAP HEIGHTS SHOWN IN FEET

GIRVAN

B734

Saugh Hill 971

Woodland Bay

Byne Hill

Mull of Miljoan 1168

Tormitchell

Mid Hill

Greensides 1098

Pindonnan Craigs

775

863

Knockdaw Hill

Colmonell

B734

Pinwherry

Ballsmore 744

612

Bennane Head

Knockdolian 193

Knockdolian Castle 871

Pinwherry Hill

Knockdhu 756

Water of Tig

BALLANTRAE BAY

B7044

Heronsford Glen Tig

Shiel Hill 752

Berthill

Laggan

Corwar Ho

Ballantrae

Balkissock

534

239

Downan Point

Glenapp Castle

Strawarren Fell

Drumlamford Druml Drumb

Currarie Port

Beneraird 1439

1041

Chimmerie

Loch Maberry

Carlock Hill 1046

538

Miljoan Hill 1321

641

Penderry Hill

Glen App

High Murdonochee

606

Milleur Point

324

Finnarts Bay

Jamieson Point

844 Mid Moile

Stab Hill 725

Craig Airie Fell

Loch Derry

Polbae

Corsewall Point

Barnhills

North Cairn

942

Standing Stones

Urrall Fell 605

South Cairn

Knockcoid

Cairn Point

Kirkcolm

The Wig

Cairnryan

A77

Lamb Hill 780

834

Quarter Fell

Eldrig Fell 742

Airie Fell 988

G

Ervie

Knocknain

Loch Corriwall 314

Braid Fell

LOCH RYAN

Balmurrie

Loch Heron

Loch Ronald

Lochnaw Castle

Leswalt

Cairnscarrow

Innermessan

11 New Luce

Glenstockadale

A718

STRANRAER

Broadsea Bay

White Loch

Aird

Lochinch Castle

Black Loch

Craig Fell 538

Drumphail

672 Bught Fell

14

Carscreugh

Castle Kennedy

Southern Upland Way

Soulseat Loch

A75

Challoch Hill 484

Dunragit

Abbey

Glenluce

Dergoals 321

Knock Moss

Black Head 356

Craigencallie Fell

Lochans 696 Cairn Pat

Genoch Mains 9 B7077

Castle of Park

A747

Whitefield Loch

430

20

Portpatrick Dunskey Castle

A77

Bean Hill

Stoneykirk

Torrs Warren

Milton

Glen of Luce

13

Castle Loch

Craignarget Hill

Doon of May

Port of Spittal Bay

B7042

Luce Sands

Chapel

Cairngarroch Bay

Money Head

Meikle Float

Sandhead

Cairngarroch

Lake Cottage

Float Bay Hole Stone Bay

Milton

Ardwell

Chapel Rossan Bay

L U C E   B A Y

Ardwell Point

A716

Balgowan Point

Logan Mains

Mull of Logan

Port Neasock or Port Logan Bay

Port Logan

Terally Point

Cairnywellan Head

400

Clanyard Bay

B7041

Kilstay Bay

Laggantalluch Head

Clanyard

Kirkmaiden

Drummore

Cailliness Point

537

Crammag Head

Damnaglaur

529

Maryport

Maryport Bay

H

Cairngaan

Scares

Port Kemin

2 MULL OF GALLOWAY

CARRICK FOREST

Lamford Hill
Dodd Hill
Cairnsmore of Carsphairn 2614
Beninner
Corlae 1906

Black Hill
Eldrick Hill
Craiglee Castle
Craigmalloch
Black Craig 2042
Garryhorn
Carsphairn B729
Knowehead
Marscalloch Hill 617
21

Pinbai
Loch Bradan Resr
1550

Loch Riecawr
Loch Macaterick
Meaul 2280
Gairy Craig
Castlemaddy
Thorny Hill
Kendoon Loch
Glenhoul
Knowehead
Culmark Hill

2521
Macaterick
1637
Tarfessock
Corserine 2669
Loch Harrow
Forrest Lodge
Carsfad Loch
Glenlee
1127

MERRICK 2766
Mullwharchar 2270
Loch Enoch
Loch Dungeon
Earlstoun Loch
Earlstoun
A702

Benyellary
L. Neldricken
2448
RHINNS OF KELLS
Cairngarroch
Drumbuie
Bennen 1249
St John's Town of Dalry
A713
Balmaclellan
B712

GLENTROOL FOREST
Glen Trool Lodge
28
Loch Trool
Loch Dee
Southern Upland Way
Garroch
Glenlee
Bogue
NEW GALLOWAY
Kenmure Castle

18 **26**
Glentrool Village
Bargrennan
Lamachan Hill 2350
Larg Hill
Darnaw
Fatteringshaws Loch
22
Cairnsmore or Black Craig of Dee
Benbrack
Ironmacannie

KIRROUGHTREE FOREST
Garlick Hill
938
1159
Brockloch Hill
Knocknevis
1067
CAIRN EDWARD FOREST
Stroan Loch
Mossdale
194

Auchinleck
Round Fell
Shaw Hill 1255
Fell of Fleet 1544
Airie Hill 955
Loch Skerrow
LAURIESTON FOREST

Garlies Castle
2331
Craigneldier
Loch Grannoch
Craiglowrie
White Top of Culreoch
636
Woodhall Loch
Lochenbreck Loch

NEWTON STEWART
Minnigaff
CAIRNSMORE OF FLEET
Clints of Dromore
1126
24
Palnure
Pibble Hill
Stey Fell
Bargatton
Loch Whinyeon

Benfield
Barraer Fell 402
High Moor of Killiemore 186
Carsegowan
Crawtown 969
Glen
Cairnharrow 1496
GLENGAP FOREST
1202
719

Spittal
Torhousemuir Stone Circle
Wigtown Sands
Carsluith Castle
Cairn Holy
10
GATEHOUSE OF FLEET
Cardoness Castle
Twynholm

WIGTOWN **5**
Bladnoch
Baldoon Sands
Ravenshall Point
Girthon
Sandgreen
A755
KIRKCUDBRIGHT

Braehead
Kirkinner
Innerwell Port
WIGTOWN BAY
Islands of Fleet
Fleet Bay
Knockbrex
Borgue
St Mary's Isle 292

Mote of Druchtag
Whauphill
Barrachan
247
Sorbie
Garlieston
Eggerness Point
Borness
Ross
Kirkcudbright Bay
Balmae

Mochrum
Drumtrodden
Monreith Mains
226
Borness Point
Little Ross
Townhead

Fell of Barhullion
Monreith
Port Allen
Portyerrock Bay
Cairn Head

WHITHORN
Priory A747
273
480
Fell of Carleton
19
St Ninian's Cave
Isle of Whithorn
St Ninian's Chapel

Point of Cairndoon
Glasserton
Port Castle Bay
BURROW HEAD

Keymap 2

SCALE 1:312 500 or 1 INCH to 5 MILES *1CM to 3.1 KM*

0   2   4   6   8   10 KILOMETRES   15

0   2   4   6 MILES   8   10

KEYMAP HEIGHTS SHOWN IN FEET

13

25

21

14

3

1

10

15

27

12

SANQUHAR

CARSPHAIRN

CARSPHAIRN FOREST

DALMACALLAN FOREST

NEW GALLOWAY
Kenmure Castle

St John's Town of Dalry

CAIRN EDWARD FOREST

LAURIESTON FOREST

GLENGAP FOREST

GATEHOUSE OF FLEET
Cardoness Castle

CASTLE DOUGLAS

DALBEATTIE

DALBEATTIE FOREST

KIRKCUDBRIGHT

Threave Castle

Crawick

Mennock

Thornhill

Penpont

Moniaive
Kirkland

Dunscore

Corsock

Springholm

Crocketford or Ninemile Bar
Milton

Old Bridge of Urr

Haugh of Urr

Mote of Urr

Clarebrand

Crossmichael

Laurieston

Townhead of Greenlaw

Parton

Bridge of Dee

Rhonehouse or Kelton Hill
Gelston

Palnackie

Screel Hill

Colvend

Kippford or Scaur

Sandyhills

Rockcliffe

Mote of Mark

Rough Island

Castlehill Point

Hestan Island

Balcary Point

Rascarrel Bay

Dundrennan
Abbey

Townhead

Borgue

Twynholm

Tongland

Ringford

Girthon

Anwoth

Sandgreen

Knockbrex

St Mary's Isle

Fleet Bay

TOWN BAY

Mansfield

Pathhead

Kirkland

Kirkland Hill

Weddle Dod

Loadhills

Wanlockhead

Lowther Hill

Conrig Hill

Stood Hill

Benty Cowan Hill

Milray Hill

Craignane

Quintin Knowe

Blackcraig Hill

White Knowes

Blacklorg Hill

Mid Hill

Corse Hill

Countam

Blackcraig Hill

Ox Hill

Cairnkinna Hill

Shiel Hill

Enterkinfoot

Durisdeer

ROMAN FORTLET

Enoch

Drumlanrig Castle

Holestane

Morton Castle

Carronbridge

Tibber's Castle

Burnhead

Closeburn

Motte of Dinning

Keir Mill

Tynron

Bogrie Hill

Wether Hill

Lochinvar

Blackcraig Hill

Barr Hill

Brockloch Hill

Shawhead

Auchenreoch Loch

Milton Loch

Lochfoot

Ironmacannie

Craig

Drumrash

Mossdale

Airie Hill

Woodhall Loch

Lochenbreck Loch

Glentoo Loch

Barcaton Loch

Carlingwark Loch

Loch Whinyeon

Loch Mannoch

Bengray

Bargatton Loch

White Top of Culreoch

Stey Fell

Craiglowrie

Loch Grannoch

Loch Skerrow

Loch Fleet

Bengairn

Barcloy Hill

Kirkcarswell

Rascarrel

Orroland

Islands of Fleet

CAIRNSMORE FOREST
Waterhead Hill

Brockloch Rig

Windy Standard

Alhang

Cairnsmore of Carsphairn

Benninner

Marscalloch Hill

Kendoon Loch

Knowehead

Culmark Hill

Trostan Loch

Glenhoul

Carsfad Loch

Earlstoun Loch

Drumbule

Garroch

Bogue

Glenlee

Benbrack

Black Water of Dee

Shaw Hill

Stroan Loch

Craigiewater

Mossdale

Keymap 2

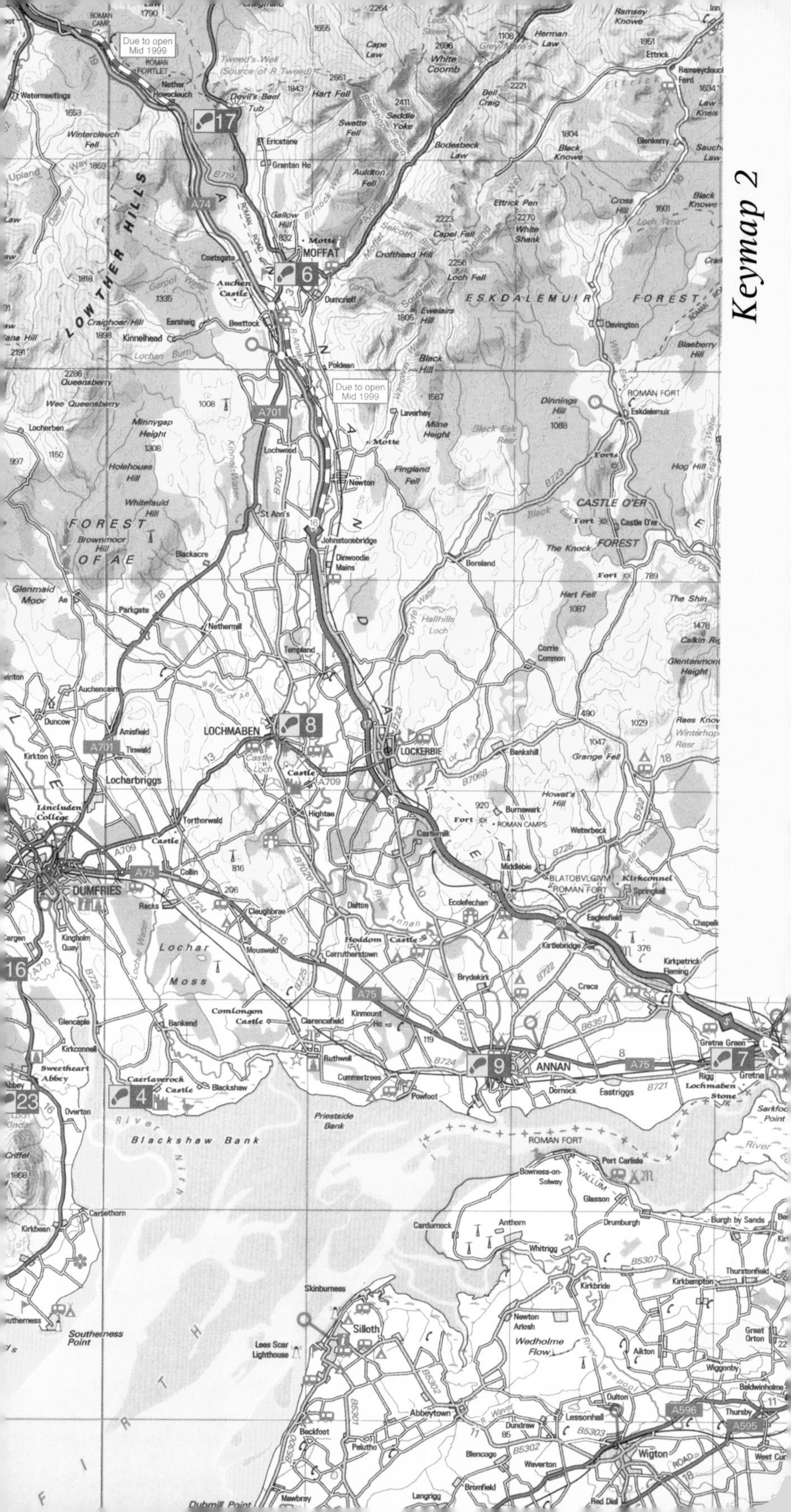

Due to open Mid 1999
Tweed's Well (Source of R Tweed)
Devil's Beef Tub
Hart Fell
White Coomb
Cape Law
Herman Law
Ramsey Knowe
Ettrick
Watermeetings
Wintercleuch Fell
Swatte Fell
Saddle Yoke
Bell Craig
Ericstane
Granton Ho
Bodesbeck Law
Black Knowe
Glenkerry
Auldton Fell
LOWTHER HILLS
Ettrick Pen
White Shank
Cross Hill
Gallow Hill
Capel Fell
Loch Fell
Coatsgate
MOFFAT
Crofthead Hill
Auchen Castle
Duncrieff
ESKDALEMUIR FOREST
Craighoar Hill
Earshaig
Beattock
Ewelairs Hill
Kinnelhead
Davington
Poldean
Black Hill
Blaeberry Hill
Queensberry
Wee Queensberry
A701
Laverhay
Milne Height
Dinnings Hill
ROMAN FORT
Eskdalemuir
Locherben
Minnygap Height
Lochwood
Motte
Holehouse Hill
Newton
Fingland Fell
Hog Hill
Whitefauld Hill
St Ann's
CASTLE O'ER FOREST
Castle O'er
FOREST OF AE
Brownmoor Hill
Johnstonebridge
Blackacre
Dinwoodie Mains
The Knock
Boreland
Glenmaid Moor
Ae
Hart Fell
The Shin
Parkgate
Nethermill
Hallhills Loch
Calkin Rig
Templand
Corrie Common
Glentenmont Height
Auchencairn
Water of Ae
Duncow
Amisfield
LOCHMABEN
Raes Knowe
Winterhope Resr
Tinwald
LOCKERBIE
Kirkton
Castle Loch
Castle
Bankshill
Grange Fell
Locharbriggs
Lincluden College
Howat's Hill
Hightae
Burnswark
ROMAN CAMPS
Torthorwald
Castlemilk
Waterbeck
DUMFRIES
Collin
Middlebie
BLATOBVLGIVM ROMAN FORT
Kirkconnel
Springkell
Racks
Cleughbrae
Dalton
Ecclefechan
Eaglesfield
Kingholm Quay
Lochar Moss
Mouswald
Hoddom Castle
Carrutherstown
Kirtlebridge
Kirkpatrick Fleming
Brydekirk
Creca
Glencaple
Bankend
Comlongon Castle
Clarencefield
Kinmount Ho
Gretna Green
Kirkconnell
Sweetheart Abbey
Ruthwell
ANNAN
Caerlaverock Castle
Blackshaw
Cummertrees
Powfoot
Rigg
Gretna
Dornock
Eastriggs
Lochmaben Stone
Overton
Priestside Bank
Sarkfoot Point
River Nith
Blackshaw Bank
Criffel
Port Carlisle
Bowness-on-Solway
VALLUM
Glasson
Carsethorn
Cardurnock
Anthorn
Drumburgh
Burgh by Sands
Kirkbean
Whitrigg
Kirkbampton
Thurstonfield
Kirkbride
Skinburness
Southerness
Southerness Point
Newton Arlosh
Silloth
Wedholme Flow
Great Orton
Lees Scar Lighthouse
Aikton
Wiggonby
FIRTH
Baldwinholme
Abbeytown
Oulton
Lessonhall
Thursby
Beckfoot
Dundraw
Pelutho
Wigton
Blencogo
West Curthwaite
Waverton
Mawbray
Langrigg
Bromfield
Red Dial
Dubmill Point
A74
A75
A709
A710
A596
A595
B719
B7020
B7068
B725
B724
B722
B723
B721
B6357
B5307
B5302
B5300
B5301
B5303
17
6
8
9
7
4
16
23

At-a-glance...

Walk	Page	Start	Distance	Time	Highest Point
Black Hill and Well Hill	76	Durisdeer	5½ miles (8.9km)	3½ hrs	1987ft (606m)
Caerlaverock and the Solway Marshes	22	Caerlaverock Castle	3½ miles (5.6km)	1½ hrs	315ft (96m)
Cairnsmore of Dee	68	Clatteringshaws Loch	6 miles (9.7km)	3½ hrs	1616ft (493m)
Cairnsmore of Fleet	73	Cairnsmore Farm	6½ miles (10.5km)	3½ hrs	2331ft (711m)
Caldons Burn and Lamachan Hill	79	Caldons Campsite	8½ miles (13.7km)	5½ hrs	2350ft (717m)
Colvend Coast	82	Kippford	10 miles (16.1km)	5 hrs	302ft (92m)
Devil's Beef Tub	56	Devil's Beef Tub	5½ miles (8.9km)	3 hrs	1569ft (4780m)
Doach Wood	16	Doach Wood	2½ miles (4km)	1½ hrs	494ft (150m)
Fleet Forest and Anwoth Old Kirk	39	Gatehouse of Fleet	5½ miles (8.9km)	3 hrs	276ft (84m)
Glenkiln Sculptures	20	Glenkiln Reservoir	4 miles (6.4km)	2 hrs	737ft (224m)
Gretna Green	30	Gretna Green	5½ miles (8.9km)	2½ hrs	131ft (40m)
Loch Trool	58	Caldons Campsite	5½ miles (8.9km)	3 hrs	525ft (160m)
Lochmaben and the Four Lochs	33	Lochmaben	5½ miles (8.9km)	2½ hrs	223ft (67m)
Mabie Forest	54	Mabie Forest	5½ miles (8.9km)	3 hrs	656ft (200m)
Manquhill Hill	66	Stroanpatrick	7½ miles (12.1km)	3½ hrs	1382ft (421m)
Merrick	86	Bruce's Stone, Loch Trool	9½ miles (15.3km)	6½ hrs	2766ft (843m)
Moffat Well and Gallow Hill	28	Moffat	4 miles (6.4km)	2 hrs	726ft (220m)
Mull of Galloway	18	Mull of Galloway	3 miles (4.8km)	1½ hrs	281ft (85m)
Portpatrick and Killantringan Fell	64	Portpatrick	8 miles (12.9km)	4 hrs	497ft (151m)
Rascarrel Bay and Balcary Point	44	Balcary Bay	5 miles (8km)	2½ hrs	166ft (50m)
St Ninian's Cave and Burrow Head	61	Kidsdale	7½ miles (12.1km)	3½ hrs	150ft (45m)
Screel Hill	52	Screel Wood	3½ miles (5.6km)	2½ hrs	1126ft (344m)
Sweetheart Abbey and Criffel	70	New Abbey	6½ miles (10.5km)	4½ hrs	1868ft (569m)
Up and Down the Annan	36	Annan	6½ miles (10.5km)	3 hrs	69ft (20m)
Wanlockhead and Lowther Hill	46	Wanlockhead	4½ miles (7.2km)	2 hrs	2378ft (725m)
Water of Ken and Garroch Glen	49	St John's Town of Dalry	4½ miles (7.2km)	2 hrs	426ft (130m)
Water of Luce and Kilhern	42	New Luce	5½ miles (8.9km)	2½ hrs	412ft (125m)
Wigtown	25	Wigtown	4½ miles (7.2km)	2 hrs	181ft (55m)

Comments

There are fine views over Nithsdale and the Lowther Hills but expect some steep and rough climbing on the first part of this walk.

For a short walk there is an immense amount of interest: splendid medieval castle, fine woodland, coastal marshes and superb views from the earthworks of a prehistoric fort.

Despite a height of only 1616 ft (493m), the latter part of the climb to the summit of Cairnsmore of Dee is very rough going. The views across Clatteringshaws Loch are outstanding.

The easiest of all the hill climbs in this guide. Pick a clear day and enjoy the superb views on both the ascent and descent.

A mixture of difficult paths – muddy and rocky – beside Caldons Burn and clear forest tracks. The extensive views from the higher points are superb.

An outstanding walk along one of the finest stretches of the Solway coast is complemented by attractive forested sections on the return leg.

This walk takes you around the edge of a deep and dramatic natural depression at the head of Annandale.

A short and easy climb through an impressive collection of Douglas firs brings you to a fine viewpoint overlooking the Solway.

A contrasting walk: attractive woodland on the first half; open, heathery moorland on the second, with a descent to a ruined church.

A series of striking sculptures by well-known sculptors in a lonely setting by a reservoir add a sense of drama to this walk.

Apart from the obvious interest of Gretna Green, the wide views across the flat lands of the Solway extend to the Southern Uplands and Cumbrian fells.

This circuit of Loch Trool in the heart of the Galloway Forest Park gives magnificent views over the surrounding mountains, including glimpses of Merrick.

This walk takes in the four lochs that surround Lochmaben and includes a visit to the ruined former castle of the Bruces.

From the forested slopes above the river Nith there are fine views of Criffel and across the Nith estuary and Solway coast.

A lonely walk with a real sense of remoteness that reveals the austere and empty landscape of the Southern Uplands at its best.

Choose a fine day and take your time. This is a lengthy and demanding walk but standing on the highest point in southern Scotland gives immense satisfaction.

Enjoy fine views of Annandale and the surrounding hills. The final stretch of the walk is a descent through lovely woodland.

Rugged cliff scenery is enjoyed on this easy circuit of the Mull of Galloway, the most southerly point in the whole of Scotland.

The first few miles of the Southern Upland Way is followed on this spectacular coastal walk. There are several climbs.

Some fine cliff scenery and grand views across the Solway are the highlights of this walk. Note that the path around Balcary Point is steep and exposed in places.

A beautiful wooded valley leads to the coast by St Ninian's Cave and this is followed by some superb cliff walking.

A steady climb through woodland leads to the summit of Screel Hill above the Solway which, despite its modest height, is a magnificent all-round viewpoint.

A beautiful ruined abbey is the start of this long, steady climb to the summit of one of the most distinctive peaks in Dumfries and Galloway.

There is attractive scenery all the way on this walk beside the River Annan from Annan to Brydekirk and back.

As well as grand views over lonely hills, there is much of interest in the former lead-mining village of Wanlockhead, the highest village in Scotland.

There are outstanding views over the Ken valley from the Southern Upland Way on the latter part of the walk.

A walk along narrow lanes and across open moorland, with dramatic views over the valley of the Water of Luce.

There are superb views across the wide expanses of Wigtown Bay and the Bladnoch estuary to the bold outlines of the Galloway hills.

Introduction to Dumfries and Galloway

Dumfries and Galloway is Scotland's south-west, a broad wedge of land jutting out into the Irish Sea between the Solway Firth and the Firth of Clyde. It is also part of Scotland's border country; from the higher points of the Galloway hills the mountains of the English Lake District can be seen rising above the opposite shores of the Solway and, in clear conditions, the hills of Northern Ireland are also visible on the skyline. Lying between the Highlands to the north and the Lake District mountains to the south, Dumfries and Galloway can get overlooked by many hillwalkers and tourists, but for those sensible enough to stop and explore, the reward is a peaceful, unspoilt region that possesses a mild climate, tremendously varied scenery and a rich historic legacy.

Mountains, Forests and Lochs

Most walkers will perhaps head for the hills and mountains of the Southern Uplands that sweep across the region before continuing eastwards into the Borders. The mountains of Dumfries and Galloway offer plenty of remote and challenging walking and there are over 40 peaks that exceed 2000 feet. The highest of these, and indeed the highest point in southern Scotland, is Merrick (2766ft/843m). The ascent of Merrick, described in Walk 28, is no mean feat and many will find it more strenuous and difficult than that of some higher peaks in other parts of the country.

Glenkiln Reservoir

On no account must the Galloway hills be underestimated. A change in the weather or decline in visibility can prove dangerous, and with often

The descent from Merrick

difficult conditions underfoot and a lack of landmarks, they should not be tackled in bad weather by any but the experienced and properly equipped. Even on the lower slopes there is often rough walking across heather, bracken and rocks with burns to ford, and few of the hills, apart from Merrick, Cairnsmore of Fleet and Criffel, have clearly defined paths leading to their summits.

The main Galloway hills can be divided into six ranges: Merrick is one of the 'fingers' that constitute 'The Awful Hand' range, so called because the individual peaks are spread out like the fingers and thumb of a hand. This is the most westerly of three parallel north–south ranges; the other two are Dungeon and the Rhinns of Kells. To the south of these is the Minnigaff group, which includes Lamachan Hill, and to the north-east is the lofty Carsphairn range. The final, more scattered, range is the Solway hills that stretch from Cairnsmore of Fleet overlooking Wigtown Bay to Criffel overlooking the Nith estuary.

Chief characteristics of the Southern Uplands are sweeping, grassy slopes rather than crags and jagged profiles, and in Dumfries and Galloway many of the lower slopes are covered by extensive conifer plantations. In the heart of the region is the Galloway Forest Park: over 300 square miles (777 sq km) of forest and moorland, mountains and lochs; a haven for wildlife with miles of waymarked trails. Further east is the Forest of Ae, and many other forests – Dalbeattie and Mabie – extend southwards to the Solway coast, all of them offering excellent walking opportunities.

Introduction

Newton Stewart

Anwoth Old Kirk

Complementing the landscape of mountains and forests is the multitude of lochs of all sizes, both natural and man-made. One of the most beautiful, and certainly the most popular, of these is Loch Trool in the heart of the Forest Park, closely associated with Robert Bruce's successful struggles to preserve Scottish independence. The paths that encircle it, featured in Walk 18, are outstandingly attractive.

Coastline, Valleys and Marshes

Away from the hills some of the most enjoyable and spectacular walking is to be found along the long and heavily indented coastline of the Solway Firth and Irish Sea. It is a varied coast with flat and marshy land at the eastern end of the Solway rising to impressively rugged cliffs further west. There is particularly fine walking along the Solway, between Kippford and Sandyhills (Walk 27), around the southern tips of the two long peninsulas of the Machars (Walk 19) and the Rhinns of Galloway (Walk 2), and along the west coast north of Portpatrick (Walk 20), the start of the Southern Upland Way.

Although there is an inevitable emphasis on hills and mountains, forests and coast, there are also several pleasant lowland walks. The wide lower valleys of the rivers Nith and Annan, the marshes of the Solway coast, and the flat expanses of the 'debatable lands' just across the English border all provide contrasting walking for those who prefer something easier and more relaxing.

Historic Heritage

Dumfries and Galloway has played a major role in some of the most momentous events in Scottish history. Scottish Christianity was born here when St Ninian established the first church in Scotland at Whithorn in AD 397. Later, a monastery was built on the site which became the cathedral of the medieval bishops of Galloway. Parts of this church survive, and two nearby sites also associated with St Ninian are the ruined chapel at Isle of Whithorn and St Ninian's Cave, the latter featured in Walk 19.

In the late 17th century the area became one of the main centres of the Covenanters Movement. The Covenanters were Presbyterians who rejected bishops and refused to accept the king as head of the Church. Many of them were persecuted and executed for their beliefs and both Walks 5 and 17 pass memorials to these martyrs.

It was among the lochs and hills of Dumfries and Galloway that Robert Bruce began the struggle to maintain Scottish independence against the ambitions of Edward I of England. The eastern part is border country and English invaders regularly used the valleys of the Nith and Annan as routeways into Scotland. The castles at Annan (Walk 9) and Lochmaben (Walk 8) were strongholds of the Bruce family and Robert Bruce's victories are commemorated at various spots throughout the region. Most notable of these is the Bruce Stone, that occupies a magnificent position overlooking Loch Trool.

Chief town of the region is Dumfries, associated with one of the most famous of Scottish literary figures. Robert Burns lived the last years of his life in the town and is buried in St Michael's church there. The other towns – Castle Douglas, Newton Stewart, Kirkcudbright, Wigtown, Moffat – are mainly small market towns and tourist centres.

Loch Trool

Routes and Weather

In Dumfries and Galloway there is plenty of variety and a wide range of walking routes to suit all ages, aptitudes and levels of fitness. Many of the walks in this guide make use of stretches of the well-

Portpatrick

waymarked Southern Upland Way, the only national trail in the region, that begins its 212 mile (340km) journey across Scotland on the west coast of Galloway. Others use hill, coastal, lochside and riverside paths and the many forest trails.

Like the other west-facing peninsulas of Britain – Cornwall, Wales, Cumbria – Dumfries and Galloway has a generally mild climate but also has its fair share of rain. Probably the best months for dry weather and sunny conditions are from April to June, but walking here is a joy at all seasons of the year. Simply choose the walk that is best suited both to your own requirements and fitness and the prevailing weather conditions, taking particular notice of the latter if you are venturing on to some of the higher hills.

Important Note

It must be stressed that although of immense scenic and recreational value, the forests of Dumfries and Galloway were planted mainly for commercial reasons and at certain times felling operations may cause the temporary closure and re-routing of some of the trails. Whenever this occurs, Forestry Commission notices will be posted at the start of the affected walks.

Introduction

Doach Wood

Start	Doach Wood, off B736 3 miles (4.8km) south-east of Castle Douglas
Distance	2½ miles (4km)
Approximate time	1½ hours
Parking	Forestry Commission car park at Doach Wood
Refreshments	None
Ordnance Survey maps	Landranger 84 (Dumfries & Castle Douglas), Pathfinders 554, NX65/75 (Kirkcudbright) and 555, NX85/95 (Dalbeattie Forest)

There are two main attractions on this short walk: the fine viewpoint along the Solway coast from the highest point and the magnificent collection of Douglas firs, especially on the latter stages. All the ascents and descents are gradual, the route is easy to follow, and the tracks and paths are firm and well-drained so that there are few muddy stretches even after prolonged rain.

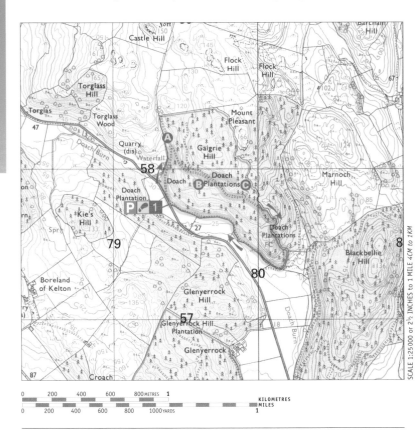

SCALE 1:25000 or 2½ INCHES to 1 MILE 4CM to 1KM

Doach Wood

Facing the wood turn left, pass beside a gate and take the steadily ascending track, following red-topped marker posts. In a short while a waterfall is seen to the left. Follow the track around a sharp right bend **Ⓐ** and continue uphill.

At the top turn left **Ⓑ** on to a path, by a red and yellow-topped post, cross a parallel track and head up to the viewpoint **Ⓒ**.

A 'Solway View' board indicates all of the many places that can be seen on a clear day from here. These include: Hestan Island, Bengairn, Screel Hill and the mountains of the English Lake District.

Retrace your steps to the track **Ⓑ** and turn left, now following yellow-topped posts for the remainder of the walk. Head gently downhill, later curving gradually to the right. The track narrows to a path which winds more steeply downhill, going round some sharp bends. On this part of the walk the Douglas firs are most impressive and there are views of the wooded slopes of Glenyerrock Hill across fields to the left as the path continues along the bottom inside edge of the wood.

On joining the red and yellow trail again there is a particularly fine display of Douglas firs on the steep hillside to the right. The path leads directly back to the car park. ●

Mull of Galloway

Start	Mull of Galloway, where road ends at the tip of the Rhinns of Galloway
Distance	3 miles (4.8km)
Approximate time	1½ hours
Parking	Mull of Galloway
Refreshments	None
Ordnance Survey maps	Landranger 82 (Stranraer & Glenluce), Pathfinder 563, NX03/04 & 13/14 (Mull of Galloway)

The Mull of Galloway, situated at the tip of the peninsula of the Rhinns of Galloway and almost detached from it, is Scotland's most southerly point. It is said that from it you can see 5 kingdoms – Scotland, England, Ireland, Isle of Man, and the Kingdom of Heaven. You can certainly see some majestic cliffs on this short and easy walk, which for the most part keeps along the edge of the cliffs. In such an exposed location, it is best to avoid this walk on windy days.

Spectacular cliffs, Mull of Galloway

SCALE 1:25000 or 2½ INCHES to 1 MILE 4CM to 1KM

Begin by going through the gate into the nature reserve to reach the southernmost tip of Scotland. Walk along a tarmac drive and where it bends right, keep ahead along a grassy track to the spectacular cliffs to the right of the lighthouse. Now follow the cliff path round to the right to return to the gate and go through it back into the car park.

Turn left, by a wall on the left, and beyond the end of the car park keep along the edge of the winding, rugged cliffs. Because of the narrowness of the peninsula, the coast is seen to both left and right.

Curve to the right to reach the neck of the peninsula – literally only a few yards wide – and by a cattle-grid turn right Ⓐ along the road.

You can follow the road back to the car park, but for a more scenic alternative bear left off the road, after climbing above an attractive bay on the left Ⓑ, and continue over the grassy cliffs.

On reaching the wall of the nature reserve Ⓒ, turn right alongside it to return to the start. ●

Glenkiln Sculptures

Start	Glenkiln Reservoir, on minor road north-west of Shawhead
Distance	4 miles (6.4km)
Approximate time	2 hours
Parking	Car park just beyond north end of Glenkiln Reservoir
Refreshments	None
Ordnance Survey maps	Landranger 84 (Dumfries & Castle Douglas), Pathfinder 529, NX87/97 (Dumfries)

As the title indicates, the main theme of this walk is a series of sculptures by a variety of well-known sculptors – Moore, Epstein, Rodin – widely scattered near the shores of Glenkiln Reservoir and on the hillside above. They were purchased and erected here by the local landowner, starting in the 1950s. Fine views across the reservoir, especially when descending Glenkiln Hill towards the end of the walk, complement the sculptures – whatever your artistic tastes may be.

The first piece of sculpture to admire, Rodin's *John the Baptist*, stands above the car park looking towards

Rodin's John the Baptist, *Glenkiln Reservoir*

the reservoir. Begin by turning right out of the car park along the lane to see Henry Moore's *Standing Figure*, by the side of the lane just before it curves right to Cornlee Bridge **Ⓐ**.

Retrace your steps and continue along the lane beside the reservoir. Moore's *Glenkiln Cross* can be seen in a commanding position on the hill to the right, and a metal gate on the right enables you to detour up to it for the superb view over the reservoir. Continue past the end of the reservoir, heading slightly downhill, and just after the lane bends right, turn right **Ⓑ** along another lane. Climb

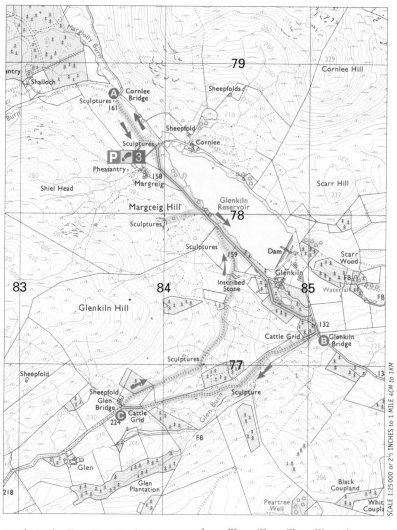

SCALE 1:25 000 or 2½ INCHES to 1 MILE 4CM to 1KM

gently to the *Two Piece Reclining Figure No. 1* by Moore, and continue past it to where the lane bears left a few yards after crossing a small burn.

Turn sharp right **C** along a clear track which recrosses a burn and later keeps by a wire fence on the left. Go through a metal gate, head gently downhill and pass to the left of Epstein's *Visitation*, a statue of the Virgin Mary situated in a small circle of pine trees.

As you continue downhill fine views open up across the reservoir and you pass to the right of a small memorial stone to Henry Moore. After going through a metal gate you reach the site of Moore's *King and Queen*, the last of the series of sculptures. Sadly, this was damaged by vandals in 1995 and at the time of writing it was being restored. It is hoped it will be re-erected in the near future.

Go through another metal gate, continue down to the lane and bear left along it to return to the start. ●

Caerlaverock and the Solway Marshes

Start	Caerlaverock Castle
Distance	3½ miles (5.6km)
Approximate time	1½ hours
Parking	Caerlaverock Castle
Refreshments	Tearoom at Caerlaverock Castle
Ordnance Survey maps	Landranger 84 (Dumfries & Castle Douglas), Pathfinder 543, NY06/16 (Annan)

A remarkable amount of historic interest and scenic diversity is packed into this short walk on the Solway coast: the extensive ruins of a medieval castle and the earthworks of its predecessor, pleasant woodland, salt-marsh, the site of an Iron Age hill fort, plus wonderful views of Criffel on the other side of the Nith estuary and across the Solway. Be prepared for wet and muddy conditions, with waterlogged paths at times, particularly on the stretch across the marshes.

Caerlaverock, one of the finest of Scottish castles, occupies an important strategic site, guarding one of the main sea routes between England and Scotland. It was built in the 1270s to replace an earlier castle on a less defensible site a few hundred yards to the south and has a triangular shape, described by one of its besiegers in 1300 as 'like a shield... surrounded by an arm of the sea'. The natural defences provided by the woods and marshes were reinforced by a moat and a powerful gatehouse built on the more exposed landward side. Captured by Edward I after a memorable siege in 1300, the castle changed hands several times and suffered much destruction and subsequent rebuilding. As a sign of more settled times, its owner Robert Maxwell, 1st Earl of Nithsdale, built an elaborate residential block in the 17th century, a fine example of Scottish Renaissance architecture, but after

Criffel from Caerlaverock Nature Reserve

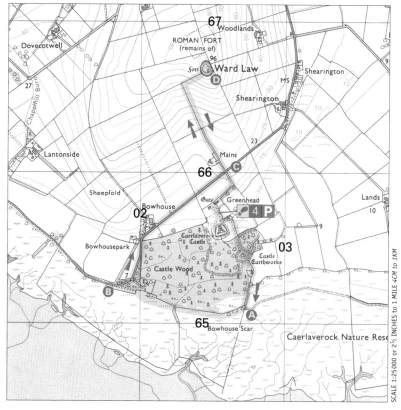

its capture by the Covenanters in 1640 the castle fell into ruin.

Begin in front of the visitor centre and take the track that passes to the left of the castle. Continue through woodland, passing a series of information boards and keeping to the left of the Old Castle earthworks.

This is the site of the first castle built in the early 13th century, abandoned after a very short life probably because it was too close to the salt-marshes.

Follow the track around right and left bends, pass to the left of two bungalows and continue – now on a path – through more attractive woodland. Cross a footbridge, keep ahead over another one and carry on across an area of grassland. On reaching a field corner, bear slightly left through a narrow belt of trees

and climb a stile on to the marshes, entering the Caerlaverock National Nature Reserve **A**.

Turn right along a waymarked path, following a series of short posts with yellow footprints, along the edge of the marsh. This is a most attractive and atmospheric part of the walk, with wide and extensive views, especially ahead across the Nith estuary to the bulk of Criffel. Climb a stile, cross a footbridge over a channel, climb another stile and continue across the marsh, eventually bearing right through trees and gorse bushes to a stile and kissing-gate side-by-side. Go through the gate and walk along a track to reach a road by a car park **B**.

Turn sharp right along the road for ¾ mile (1.2km) to the sign on the right for Caerlaverock Castle **C**.

You can turn right for a quick return, but for a brief and worthwhile detour to the fort and viewpoint of Ward Law, turn left through a metal gate and walk along a track. Ahead is a view of Ward Law crowned by trees. Go through another metal gate, continue steadily uphill along the left edge of a field and in the top corner turn right to keep along the field edge up to Ward Law **D**.

A ladder-stile gives access to the earthworks of this Iron Age hill fort, not only of interest as the first of several fortifications in this area, but also for the fine collection of trees (mainly beeches) that now crown the site and the magnificent views. The latter extend over the Solway to the Cumbrian mountains, across the River Nith to Criffel, and inland to the line of the Southern Uplands. Below, the castle, woods and marshes are clearly visible.

Retrace your steps to the road **C**, cross over and take the tarmac drive opposite to return to the start. ●

Magnificent Caerlaverock Castle

Wigtown

Start	Wigtown
Distance	4½ miles (7.2km). Shorter versions 2 miles (3.2km) and 2½ miles (4km)
Approximate time	2 hours (1 hour for each of the shorter versions)
Parking	Wigtown
Refreshments	Pubs and cafés at Wigtown
Ordnance Survey maps	Landranger 83 (Newton Stewart & Kirkcudbright), Pathfinder 553, NX45/55 (Wigtown)

This pleasant, easy-paced, figure-of-eight walk around the small town of Wigtown can easily be split into two separate shorter walks. There are several reminders of Wigtown's history on the route and from many points you can enjoy superb views across the wide expanses of Wigtown Bay to the outline of the Galloway hills on the horizon.

Wigtown is a place of past glories. Once an important royal burgh, port and route centre, with a harbour, castle and monastery, it is now a sleepy backwater. The huge, triangular open space in the town centre, where the walk begins, is a reminder of its former greatness.

Start at the Mercat Cross where the wide main street divides and take the left-hand street (North Main Street). Pass to the left of the Town Hall and follow the street down to the 19th-century church. Adjoining the church are the ruins of its 18th-century predecessor and in the churchyard are the Martyrs' Graves.

The martyrs were two local women, Margaret McLaughlin and Margaret Wilson, executed in 1685 for supporting the Covenanters, ie. people who refused to accept the king as head of the Scottish Church. They were tied to a stake in the estuary of the River Bladnoch and drowned by the rising waters as the tide came in.

The stones in the churchyard are probably a memorial rather than a grave as executed Covenanters were denied proper burial for fear that they would become recognised as martyrs.

Continue past the church to a small car park and a sign 'Martyrs Stake', and turn right Ⓐ along a track signposted to Wigtown Harbour. A boardwalk on the left leads to the stake, erected on the supposed site where the two women were drowned. Continue along the enclosed track, go through a kissing-gate and keep ahead to reach a metal gate. Do not go through the gate but turn left down to a stile, climb the stile and continue along a raised embankment above the marshes, a National Nature Reserve. This is a lovely part of the walk with fresh sea breezes and expansive views across Wigtown Bay to the Galloway hills.

Follow the embankment as it curves first right and then left, climb a stile and turn right to continue

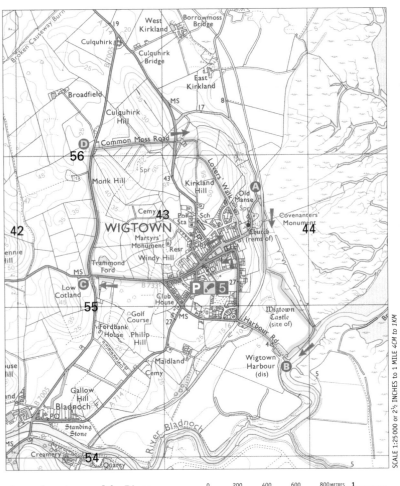

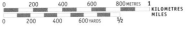

above the estuary of the River Bladnoch. Now there are pleasant views of the town on the low hill to the right.

Climb a stile and go down steps to the site of the former harbour. Walk through the car park and turn right along a lane **B**. In the fields to the right is the site of Wigtown's medieval castle.

On reaching a road at a bend, turn right up Harbour Road and turn left along South Main Street, passing to the left of the Town Hall, to return to the starting point.

For the second part of the figure-of-eight, continue past the Mercat Cross and take the road ahead, signposted to Kirkcowan. On the hill to the right is the Martyrs' Monument, erected in 1858 in memory of the Wigtown Martyrs. At a crossroads turn right **C**, in the Newton Stewart direction – take care as this is a busy road – and after ½ mile (800m) turn right again **D** on to a straight, enclosed track. The track, later tree-lined, ascends gently to a road.

Cross over the road and at a footpath sign 'Wigtown via Lovers' Walk' keep ahead along a tarmac drive and go through a gate to the left of a bungalow. Now comes a succession of superb views across the bay as you continue gently uphill along a grassy, tree-lined, enclosed track. The track bends right and at a junction of tracks, turn left along another enclosed track. On reaching the edge of the town, continue down a road to a T-junction and then turn right uphill to return to the start. ●

Wigtown Bay

Moffat Well and Gallow Hill

Start	Moffat
Distance	4 miles (6.4km)
Approximate time	2 hours
Parking	Moffat
Refreshments	Pubs and cafés at Moffat
Ordnance Survey maps	Landranger 78 (Nithsdale & Annandale), Pathfinder 495, NT00/10 (Moffat)

From the centre of Moffat the route heads gently uphill to Moffat Well, a pleasant spot where Birnock Water tumbles through a narrow, wooded ravine. The return is an attractive and easy descent through the woodlands that clothe Gallow Hill. There are fine views of the encircling hills and across Upper Annandale.

The fountain surmounted by a statue of a ram in the centre of Moffat's unusually wide High Street symbolises the town's history as an important wool centre. In the 18th and 19th centuries the town also became a very popular spa and the Town Hall once housed the baths and pump room. Moffat's attractive location in Upper Annandale and wide assortment of hotels, guest houses, shops, inns and cafés makes the town an excellent touring and walking centre.

Annandale from Gallow Hill

Start in front of the Town Hall and with your back to it turn right along High Street. By the war memorial turn left along Well Street, turn right along Well Road and follow it out of town. After just over ¹/₂ mile (800m), bear right Ⓐ along Alton Road – a narrow, hedge-lined lane.

The lane continues as a track which winds gently uphill. Keep to the right of a large house, follow the track around left and right bends and pass between farm buildings to a gate. Go through, keep above a burn on the right and where the track crosses a bridge over the burn, turn left through a kissing-gate.

Bear right gently uphill across the corner of a field to go through a metal gate and head straight across the next field to a kissing-gate. Go through that, continue, soon picking up a recognisable track and go through a metal gate to cross a bridge over Birnock Water. The track now winds uphill to go through another metal gate on to a lane to the right of a bridge Ⓑ.

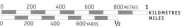

Turn right up the lane for ¼ mile (400m) to Moffat Well, reached by turning right through a parking and picnic area and going through a gate. The well was one of a number in the area that helped to make Moffat a popular health resort.

Retrace your steps down the lane to the bridge Ⓑ, cross it and where the lane bends left, turn right through a metal gate and walk along a track. Pass to the left of a line of barns and go through another metal gate. Continue gently uphill, go through a metal gate, keep ahead and the track swings left Ⓒ to continue beside the wall just crossed. On reaching the edge of woodland, turn left through a metal gate and take the path through conifers to meet a track.

Turn right and follow the track downhill through Gallowhill Wood. At a fork turn right, go through a metal kissing-gate, cross a track and go through another metal kissing-gate. The track bends left and now comes a splendid finale to the walk as you continue down Gallow Hill through delightful broad-leaved woodland. Attractive views over Annandale can be seen through gaps in the trees on the right.

At a fork either track will do – they later rejoin and run parallel – but the right-hand track probably gives the best views. Eventually you join another track by Beechwood Country House Hotel and continue downhill. The track becomes a road which bends to the right, passing to the right of St Mary's church, to the main road. Turn left in front of the church to return to the start. ●

Gretna Green

Start	Gretna Green
Distance	5½ miles (8.9km). Shorter version 3 miles (4.8km)
Approximate time	2½ hours (1½ hours for shorter version)
Parking	Gretna Green, The Old Blacksmith's Shop Visitor Centre
Refreshments	Hotels, restaurants and café at Gretna Green
Ordnance Survey maps	Landranger 85 (Carlisle & Solway Firth), Pathfinder 544, NY26/36 (Gretna & Eastriggs)

For many centuries the flat lands of the Solway plain were the 'debatable lands', constantly fought over and changing hands between Scottish and English kings until the Union of Crowns in 1603 brought some peace to this troubled border area. This easy and relaxing walk gives wide views across the flat country to the Southern Uplands, Criffel and across the Solway to the mountains of the Lake District. The shorter version returns more directly to Gretna Green.

For nearly 200 years Gretna Green was the most famous place in Britain for runaway marriages and romantic elopements. There were two main reasons for this. In 1754 Parliament passed an Act which prevented secret marriages without parental consent in England but not in Scotland, and Gretna Green was the first village across the border on one of the main stage coach routes between England and Scotland. Traditionally, many of these secret marriages took place over a blacksmith's anvil and the walk starts in front of the Old Blacksmith's Shop Marriage Room.

Take the lane to the right, signposted to Corries Mill, and opposite a lane on the right, turn left Ⓐ, at a public footpath sign, along a hedge- and partially tree-lined track. The track bends right to pass under a railway bridge, Quintinshill Bridge,

scene in 1915 of Britain's worst rail disaster. Over 220 people were killed and many more were injured in a multiple collision.

Continue along the track and at a footpath sign to Springfield and Gretna Green, turn left Ⓑ along a tarmac track to a lane. Turn left, cross a railway bridge and walk along the lane as far as the corner of a small wood on the left Ⓒ.

Here the shorter version of the walk continues along the lane to return to Gretna Green.

For the full walk, turn right along a straight, hedge-lined track which bends left to reach a road. Turn right, take the first turning on the left Ⓓ to cross the M74 and follow the road to the left towards a service area. Opposite the Forte Travelodge, turn right down a tarmac drive and at a fork a few yards ahead, take the

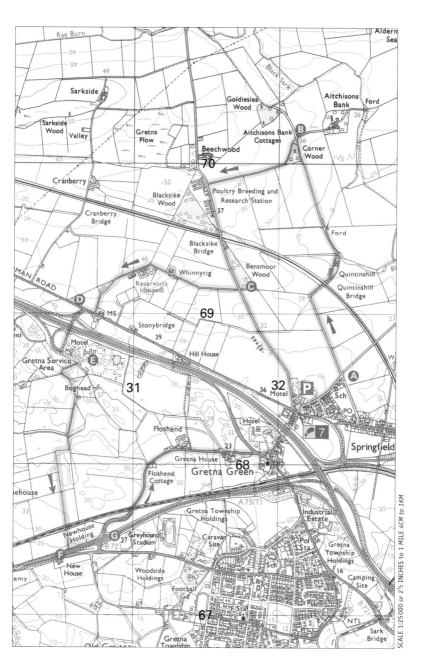

right-hand track **E**. Go through a kissing-gate and continue gently uphill. From here there are fine views of Criffel ahead and to the left the outline of the Cumbrian mountains on the other side of the Solway.

The track bends first left and then right and at the right bend, turn left along a grassy track, partially enclosed but with a wire fence and hedge on the right all the time. Go through a metal gate, keep ahead to go through another metal gate and turn right along the right edge of a field. Follow the field edge round to the left, continue to a metal gate, go through and keep along the left edge of the next field, by a hedge and wire fence on the left. Climb a stile, cross a railway bridge, go through a metal gate and continue along the right edge of a field to climb a stile on to a road **F**.

Turn left, take the first turning on the left **G**, signposted 'Gretna Green and Springfield', recross the railway and continue into Gretna Green. At a T-junction turn right and almost immediately turn left, opposite the Old Kirk, and follow the road under the motorway back to the start. ●

The Old Blacksmith's Shop Marriage Room

Lochmaben and the Four Lochs

Start	Lochmaben
Distance	5½ miles (8.9km).Shorter version 3½ miles (5.6km)
Approximate time	2½ hours (1½ hours for shorter version)
Parking	Lochmaben
Refreshments	Pubs and cafés at Lochmaben
Ordnance Survey maps	Landranger 78 (Nithsdale & Annandale), Pathfinder 518, NY08/18 (Lockerbie & Lochmaben)

The town of Lochmaben in Annandale is surrounded by four lochs – Upper, Mill, Kirk and Castle – and on the south side of Castle Loch, the largest of the four, stand the ruins of a medieval castle. This walk either passes or provides views of all of them and the castle is the main focal point. It is a flat and easy walk that can be done at any time of the year and there are some splendid views across the lochs. The shorter version omits the walk to the castle ruins.

Lochmaben is very much a one-street town: at the top end of High Street is the town hall with a statue of Robert the Bruce in front, and at the bottom end is the church.

Start by the Bruce statue, walk down High Street and in front of the church turn right **Ⓐ** along Mounsey's Wynd to a T-junction. In front is Castle Hill, the motte of the original 12th-century castle of the Bruces and predecessor of the one on the shores of Castle Loch. Turn left at a Scottish Rights of Way Society public footpath sign and go along a tarmac track. To the right is a golf course and view of Kirk Loch.

*If doing the shorter walk, turn right through a gate **Ⓑ** at a public footpath sign just before reaching a farm.*

For the full walk continue along the track, passing to the left of the

farm, and go through a metal gate. Continue along the right edge of a field, by a hedge and wire fence on the right, and in the corner follow the field edge to the left and climb a stepladder stile on to a road. Turn right and at a sign for Lochmaben Castle, turn left **Ⓒ** along a tarmac drive. After passing a farm entrance, the drive becomes a rough track. Follow it to the left through a kissing-gate into woodland to reach the remains of the castle **Ⓓ**.

Fragmentary though the remains are, Lochmaben Castle has had an interesting and, inevitably for a Border castle occupying an important strategic route between England and Scotland, troubled history. It belonged to the Bruce family, after they abandoned the earlier castle in the centre of the town, though the

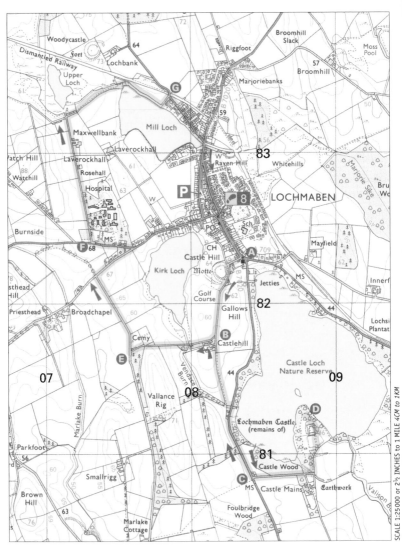

first castle on the site was probably built by Edward I in 1298 while on one of his many invasions of Scotland. Lochmaben Castle frequently changed hands and suffered destruction in the almost constant Border warfare, and most of the present remains date from a 14th-century rebuilding. The castle lies in an attractive setting and paths lead down through the trees to the shores of Castle Loch, a nature reserve.

Retrace your steps to the farm at Castle Hill and at the public footpath sign, turn left through a gate Ⓑ, to rejoin the shorter route. Walk along a path, enjoying views across the golf course of Kirk Loch on the right.

Go through another gate, continue, between a conifer wood on the left and a wall bordering a cemetery on the right, and go through a kissing-gate on to a lane Ⓔ. Turn right, and at a T-junction turn right again to a road on the edge of the town and turn sharp left along it. Take the first turning on the right Ⓕ, at a 'No

Through Road' sign, and continue along a straight, narrow lane.

Where the lane ends at a T-junction of tracks, there is a view of Upper Loch ahead. Turn right, passing in front of cottages, go through a kissing-gate and keep ahead across grass to pick up and keep beside a wire fence – later a hedge – on the right. Now come fine views to the right of Mill Loch and the town beyond. Near the end of the field, bear left to a kissing-gate and public footpath sign in the left-hand corner, go through and keep ahead, by a wire fence on the left.

The path curves right and continues through trees that line the shores of Mill Loch. Bear left uphill, now along a track, to a road and turn right Ⓖ into Lochmaben. Turn right at a T-junction across the end of the loch, and at a fork, take the left-hand road to return to the start. ●

Lochmaben Castle

Up and Down the Annan

Start	Annan
Distance	6½ miles (10.5km). Shorter versions 2 miles (3.2km) and 3½ miles (5.6km)
Approximate time	3 hours (1 hour and 1½ hours for shorter versions)
Parking	Annan
Refreshments	Pubs and cafés at Annan, pub at Brydekirk
Ordnance Survey maps	Landranger 85 (Carlisle & Solway Firth), Pathfinder 543, NY06/16 (Annan)

With an understandable emphasis on hill, lochside, forest and coastal walking in this book, it makes a pleasant change to include a wholly riverside walk, especially such an attractive stretch of the River Annan. The route could hardly be easier to follow: upstream along the east bank from Annan to Brydekirk and downstream along the west bank, and the two bridges passed before reaching Brydekirk enable you to shorten the walk at will.

In the 12th century Annan was one of the chief strongholds of the Bruce family and the motte or mound of their former castle is passed near the start of the walk. Later, it became a fishing and shipbuilding centre.

Begin in the main street and facing the impressive red sandstone town hall, walk along the road to the left of it and turn right down Battery Street

The River Annan

to the entrance to Everholm Park **Ⓐ**. Immediately there is a fine view upstream.

Go through a gate and take the tarmac riverside path through the park. To the right is the castle motte. Where the tarmac path ends, pass through a wall gap and keep beside the river up to the road bridge at Brydekirk. En route you pass two footbridges – first a metal one and secondly a suspension bridge.

*Cross either bridge for the two shorter walks and return to the start (see text after **Ⓒ**, below).*

The undulating path passes through a mixture of woodland and meadows, goes under the Annan bypass, crosses several footbridges over tributary burns and negotiates a number of kissing-gates and stiles.

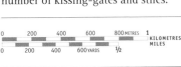

Approaching Brydekirk the river flows between steep wooded banks, a most attractive stretch of the walk.

At the bridge turn left **B** and by the Brig Inn turn left again along a lane. Where the lane bends right, keep ahead **C** along the riverside path to follow the other bank back to Annan across the same mixture of woodland and meadow. The only slight complication is that soon after passing the metal footbridge (the second one), continue along a track but look out for where the track bears slightly right. At this point bear left off it to continue along a narrow riverside path.

As you approach Annan there are grand views of the town. Finally, climb a flight of steps by Annan Bridge and turn left over it **D** to return to the start.

Along the river

Fleet Forest and Anwoth Old Kirk

Start	Gatehouse of Fleet
Distance	5½ miles (8.9km). Shorter versions 2 miles (3.2km) and 3½ miles (5.6km)
Approximate time	3 hours (1 hour and 2 hours for shorter versions)
Parking	Gatehouse of Fleet
Refreshments	Pubs and cafés at Gatehouse of Fleet
Ordnance Survey maps	Landranger 83 (Newton Stewart & Kirkcudbright), Pathfinders 554, NX65/75 (Kirkcudbright) and 553, NX45/55 (Wigtown)

This figure-of-eight walk can be divided into two separate shorter walks if desired. The two halves of the walk are completely different. The first half is a flat and easy walk mainly through the attractive woodland of Fleet Forest, and the second half, after initially climbing to a fine viewpoint above the town, is a hillier route across the heather- and bracken-covered slopes of Boreland Hill.

Pleasantly situated on the Water of Fleet, the main street of Gatehouse of Fleet is dominated by a tall 19th-century clock tower. The Mill on the Fleet, a former cotton mill by the river, is now an exhibition centre featuring the history of the town and local area.

From the car park turn right along the main street and opposite Digby Street, turn right again under an arch, at a sign 'Footpath to Public Park'. Walk first along a track and then along a path which crosses a bridge over a burn and continues into a recreation ground. Turn left along a track by the edge of the recreation ground, pass beside a gate and the track curves right to a T-junction Ⓐ.

Turn right along a tarmac drive, keep ahead to pass beside a gate and continue along what is now a rough track into woodland. At a crossroads of tracks keep ahead, in the Dalavan direction, and after a few yards you pick up the white, yellow and blue-topped posts of a forest trail. Look out for where a post directs you to turn right on to a winding path.

Cross a footbridge over a burn, keep ahead at the next post, pass a white and yellow-topped post and head up to a T-junction of paths. Turn right and the path emerges on to a tarmac drive Ⓑ.

Turn right and take the first track on the left, signposted Cricket Ground. The track curves left, heads gently downhill and bears right to cross a burn. Follow the track to the left and a few yards before it crosses another burn and bends right, turn sharp right on to a path **C**. After crossing a burn the path turns left to keep beside it. Cross a track and keep ahead to meet a track at a U-bend just in front of the recreation ground. Take the left-hand track to the river and cross a footbridge over a burn. Keep ahead, go through a gate and walk across a picnic area to return to the car park.

For the second part of the figure-of-eight, turn left out of the car park and cross the bridge over the Water of Fleet. Where the road bears left, turn right **D** through a kissing-gate, at a National Trust for Scotland sign 'Venniehill'. For a short detour, follow a winding grassy path uphill – plenty of yellow waymarks – to a toposcope and a viewpoint over the town, Fleet Forest and the surrounding hills.

Descend to the road **D** and turn left along a lane. The lane curves left uphill and by a cattle-grid, bear slightly left to go through a metal gate at a public footpath sign. Walk along a narrow path, between a wall on the right and trees on the left, go through a gate and climb first a stone stile and immediately after another stile. Turn right, continue uphill across a grassy slope dotted with trees and then follow a winding path – looking out for yellow waymarks – across the gorse, heather and bracken of Boreland Hill.

The waymarks peter out and there are a number of paths, but two prominent features seen on the skyline ahead are your landmarks: the Rutherford Monument and a triangulation pillar.

First make your way up to the monument **E**, a superb viewpoint

The view from Boreland Hill

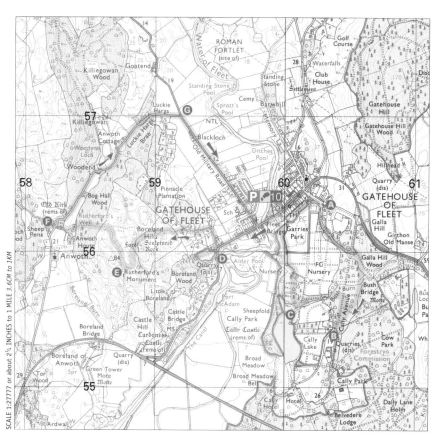

SCALE 1:27777 or about 2¼ INCHES to 1 MILE 3.6CM to 1KM

overlooking the Fleet estuary and
Wigtown Bay. It was erected in 1842
in memory of Samuel Rutherford, a
17th-century scholar, religious
teacher and minister at nearby
Anwoth church.

At the monument turn right and
head across to the triangulation pillar
for more grand views. Continue in
the same direction, down into a dip
and up again, and descend through
bracken to a wall bordering
woodland. On meeting an obvious
track, turn left through a metal gate
in the wall and follow the track
steeply downhill through conifers. Go
through another metal gate on the
edge of the trees and ahead is
Anwoth Old Kirk. Bear left across a
field, go through a metal gate at the
corner of the churchyard wall, walk

along a path and go through a metal
gate on to a lane **F**.

The atmospheric ruins of the Old
Kirk date from the 17th century and
the church remained in use until the
early 19th century when it was
replaced by the new church about
¼ mile (400m) to the south. The
tower of the new church will have
been clearly seen from the
triangulation pillar.

Turn right along the lane in front
of the Old Kirk and follow it for
nearly 1 mile (1.6km) to a T-junction
G. Turn right along a road back into
Gatehouse of Fleet and at a
T-junction turn left over Fleet Bridge
to return to the start. ●

Water of Luce and Kilhern

Water of Luce and Kilhern

Start	New Luce
Distance	5½ miles (8.9km)
Approximate time	2½ hours
Parking	Roadside parking in New Luce
Refreshments	Pub at New Luce
Ordnance Survey maps	Landranger 82 (Stranraer & Glenluce), Pathfinder 538, NX06/16 (Stranraer & New Luce)

About half the walk is along quiet roads and narrow lanes in the lush valley of the Water of Luce. The remainder follows a section of the Southern Upland Way across expanses of open, heathery moorland, more reminiscent perhaps of parts of the Pennines than the rest of Galloway. On the descent from the prehistoric burial chamber at Kilhern back into the valley, the views are particularly memorable.

The quiet village of New Luce is attractively situated where the Main Water of Luce and the Cross Water of Luce unite to form the Water of Luce.

Start by the Southern Upland Way information shelter at the T-junction in the village centre and walk southwards, in the Glenluce direction. Cross a bridge over the Cross Water

Moorland near New Luce

of Luce, pass to the right of the church and continue along the road for 1¼ miles (2km). There are very pleasant views to the right across the valley.

At a Southern Upland Way sign opposite a farm entrance on the right Ⓐ, turn left over a ladder-stile and take an uphill track. On reaching three metal gates, climb a stile beside the middle one of the three and walk along the left edge of a field, by a wall on the left, to climb another ladder-stile.

Ahead are three tracks: continue along the middle one which heads in a straight line across open moorland for 1¾ miles (2.8km). Climb a ladder-stile, keep ahead and on approaching the ruined farm at Kilhern, follow

the direction of a Southern Upland Way post to the left **B**.

Keep by a wall on the right, pass through a wall gap and at another waymarked post, turn left to continue across the moorland. Climb a ladder-stile and over to the right are the Caves of Kilhern, a Neolithic burial chamber probably constructed around 2000-3000 years ago. The path now starts to descend, there are fine and extensive views ahead over the valley and the terrain changes from rough, heathery moorland to smoother grassland. Keep by the wall on the right all the while, passing a conifer plantation, and after the wall ends continue to a Southern Upland Way post.

Turn left along a track down to a lane and turn left **C** along this narrow lane, heading gently downhill to the church at New Luce. At a T-junction by the church, turn right to return to the start. ●

Rascarrel Bay and Balcary Point

Start	Balcary Bay, at end of minor road from Auchencairn
Distance	5 miles (8km)
Approximate time	2½ hours
Parking	Balcary Bay
Refreshments	None
Ordnance Survey maps	Landranger 84 (Dumfries & Castle Douglas), Pathfinders 555, NX85/95 (Dalbeattie Forest) and 565, NX64/74 (Kirkcudbright Bay)

*From Balcary Bay the first part of the route heads inland –
across fields, beside an attractive loch and through a conifer
plantation – to rejoin the coast at Rascarrel Bay. The rest of the
walk follows the coast, initially along the edge of a stony beach,
later climbing on to low cliffs and finally rounding the steep and
dramatic headland of Balcary Point, the scenic highlight of the
walk. On this last stretch comes a succession of spectacular
views over Auchencairn Bay and across the Solway Firth to the
Cumbrian mountains.*

From the car park take the tarmac track signposted 'Right of Way to Loch Mackie and Rascarrel Bay'. Where the main track bears left, keep ahead – at a footpath sign – along a rough track, passing to the right of a house.

Go through a metal gate, keep along the track by a wall on the left, but after going through a kissing-gate the route continues along a narrow path beside Loch Mackie. Cross a footbridge and bear first left and then right to continue through woodland, now along a track again, to reach a lane Ⓐ.

Turn left and after ½ mile (800m), turn left again Ⓑ, at a footpath sign 'Right of Way to Rascarrel Bay', along a hedge- and tree-lined track.

The track continues beside the stony shore of Rascarrel Bay and after passing in front of some cottages, narrows to a path.

Later, the path climbs on to low cliffs and continues to a metal kissing-gate. Go through and now comes a series of spectacular and ever-changing views, across the Solway and later over Auchencairn Bay to Hestan Island and the coast beyond, as the path rounds the rocky headland of Balcary

Balcary Bay

Point. On this part of the walk there are some steep climbs and there are notices warning you to take care as at times the path comes very close to the cliff edge.

After rounding the point, continue through attractive woodland to a kissing-gate **C**. Go through, keep along the right edge of a field – variously trees, wall and a wire fence on the right – pass to the left of a house and bear right in the field corner to go through another kissing-gate. Walk along an enclosed track to return to the start. ●

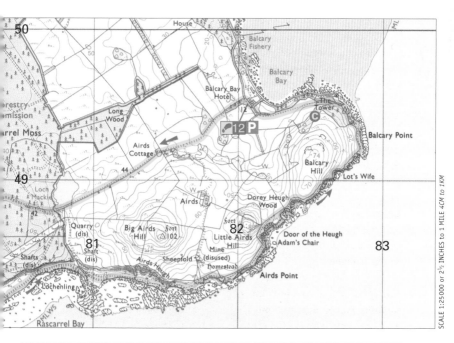

Wanlockhead and Lowther Hill

Start	Wanlockhead
Distance	4½ miles (7.2km)
Approximate time	2 hours
Parking	Museum of Lead Mining car park at Wanlockhead
Refreshments	Café at Museum of Lead Mining Visitor Centre
Ordnance Survey maps	Landrangers 71 (Lanark & Upper Nithsdale) and 78 (Nithsdale & Annandale), Pathfinder 482, NS81/91 (Leadhills)

The route follows a section of the Southern Upland Way southwards from the village of Wanlockhead to the summit of Lowther Hill (2378ft/725m), easily distinguished by the masts and 'golf balls' of the radar station there. The climb is a continuous and steady one across the grassy slopes of the hill, made considerably easier by the starting point being at over 1500ft (457m). On both the ascent and descent there are wide and extensive views over the surrounding hills. It is advisable not to attempt this walk in misty weather.

The old lead mining village of Wanlockhead, 1531ft (466m) high, is Scotland's highest village, and cradled by the bare and lonely Lowther Hills, it is both uniquely interesting and highly atmospheric. Lead has been mined in the area since the 13th century but mining activity was at its height in the 18th and 19th centuries and the last mines closed in the 1950s. The whole place is an outdoor living museum and it is worthwhile following a trail from the visitor centre that takes you down a mine and into miners' cottages, past a spoil heap, smelt mills

and a beam engine, enabling you to get some idea of what life was like in this isolated community in the heyday of the mines.

Start the walk by climbing the flight of steps that lead off from the end of the museum car park. Head

Wanlockhead

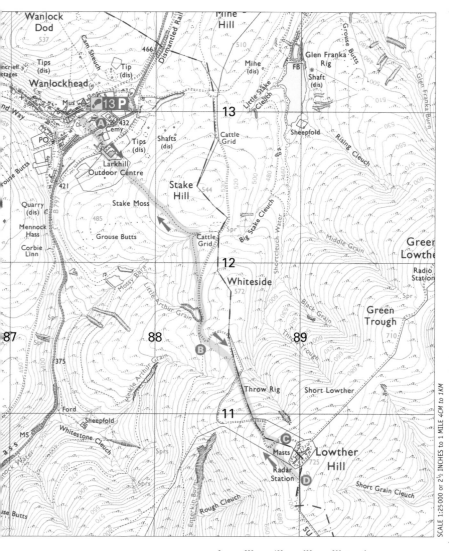

SCALE 1:25000 or 2½ INCHES to 1 MILE 4CM to 1KM

across the grass, cross a stony track and continue along a grassy track to a road Ⓐ.

Cross over the road, take the uphill track opposite and cross a disused railway track by the former Wanlockhead station.

Continue uphill, by a wire fence on the right, and where the fence ends, follow the clear track ahead across the heathery hillside.

Turn right to cross a footbridge over a burn and continue up to the road which winds up to the radar station, erected by the Ministry of Civil Aviation on the summit of Lowther Hill in 1948. This road is crossed several times as, fortunately, the Southern Upland Way takes a more direct route.

Turn right along the road but at a sharp left-hand bend Ⓑ, continue along the path which can clearly be seen ahead, the route marked with regular Southern Upland Way posts.

Recross the road, continue uphill, by a wire fence on the left, cross the road on two more occasions and eventually join it again just to the right of the radar station.

Turn right **C** along the road as far as a right-hand bend where you turn left and head across grass to climb a stile on the right in front of the radar station masts and 'golf balls'. Turn left and continue in the same direction to reach a stile in a wire fence just below the summit **D**. There are superb all-round views from here across the rolling, empty Lowther Hills, and looking down the length of Nithsdale the Solway Firth can be seen in the distance.

From here retrace your steps downhill back to the start. ●

The old school at Wanlockhead

Water of Ken and Garroch Glen

Start	St John's Town of Dalry
Distance	4½ miles (7.2km)
Approximate time	2 hours
Parking	Roadside parking in centre of St John's Town of Dalry
Refreshments	Pubs and cafés at St John's Town of Dalry
Ordnance Survey maps	Landranger 77 (Dalmellington to New Galloway), Pathfinder 516, NX68/78 (St John's Town of Dalry), Outdoor Leisure Map 32 (Galloway Forest Park)

The walk begins by crossing the Water of Ken and continues along a quiet and pleasant lane through Garroch Glen. Then follows an easy and gentle climb over Waterside Hill that provides you with a series of outstandingly attractive views over the Ken valley and St John's Town of Dalry as you descend back to the start.

St John's Town of Dalry – Dalry for short – beautifully situated above the Water of Ken, is only a village in size but it has the feel and appearance of a small town. The close proximity of the town hall, the motte of a 12th-

St John's Town of Dalry

century castle, and church help to create this impression. The church, seen prominently on the latter stages of the walk, was built in 1831 and beside it is the ruined Gordon Aisle of its medieval predecessor, former burial place of the Gordons of nearby Lochinvar.

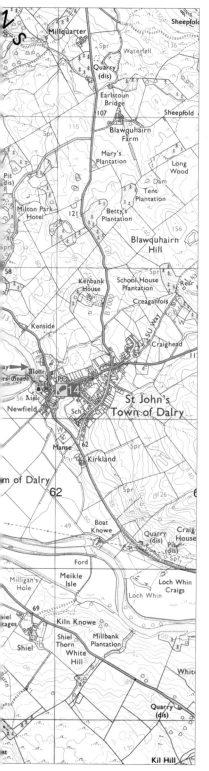

The walk starts by the fountain in the town centre. Take the track to the right of the town hall, at a Southern Upland Way fingerpost, and continue along a path which descends to the Water of Ken. The castle motte is to the right and the church to the left.

Cross the suspension footbridge over the river, turn left down steps and keep ahead between gorse bushes. Follow a Southern Upland Way marker post to the right, continue across a field and climb a ladder-stile on to a road **A**.

Turn left and cross two bridges over channels of Coom Burn to reach a T-junction **B**. Turn right and follow a quiet lane through Garroch Glen, passing to the right of Glenlee Water Power Station, built in 1934. After 1½ miles (2.4km) turn right **C**, at a Southern Upland Way fingerpost, along a narrow path through trees.

The path bears right beside Garroch Burn, turns left to cross a footbridge over it and turns right to keep parallel to a wall on the right. Continue through a wooded area, cross another footbridge and climb a ladder-stile. Now follow a series of waymarked posts across a rocky field, likely to be boggy in places, climbing over Waterside Hill. At the top of the hill comes the first of a series of superb views over the Ken valley.

Descend gently, picking up and keeping by a wall on the right, and head down to go through a gate in the bottom corner of a field. Follow an enclosed path down to a road – to the left is another water power station – and turn right **D** along it. At a Southern Upland Way fingerpost turn left **A** over a ladder-stile and retrace your steps to the start. ●

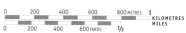

Screel Hill

Start	Forestry Commission's Screel Wood car park, about 200 yds (183m) along minor road to left off A711, 2 miles (3.2km) north of Auchencairn
Distance	3½ miles (5.6km)
Approximate time	2½ hours
Parking	Screel Wood
Refreshments	None
Ordnance Survey maps	Landranger 84 (Dumfries & Castle Douglas), Pathfinders 554, NX65/75 (Kirkcudbright) and 555, NX85/95 (Dalbeattie Forest)

Screel Hill rises to the north of the village of Auchencairn and, despite its modest height of 1126ft (344m), the summit provides grand, extensive and uninterrupted views over the Galloway hills and along the Solway coast. The route follows a well-waymarked Forestry Commission trail and the climb is a steady one, though near the top the going becomes steeper and rockier. The descent is very easy and straightforward. Do not attempt this walk in bad weather and misty conditions unless experienced in such conditions and able to navigate by using a compass.

Pass beside the gate at the end of the car park, in the 'Screel Hill Walk' direction, and follow a winding, steadily ascending track through conifers. The entire walk is waymarked with white-ringed posts but you do need to keep a sharp look out for them.

Where the track forks, keep ahead – bisecting the fork – along a much narrower uphill path through an area of dark, tightly-packed, gloomy conifers. The path emerges on to a track Ⓐ, cross it and continue uphill, passing to the right of a bench from which there is a fine view over the Solway. Head up through the trees and after crossing a footbridge, turn left to reach a reassuring waymark. Eventually you emerge from the forest into an open area of bracken and heather.

Continue more steeply now along a rocky path, keeping to the left of a line of crags. Bengairn is the wooded hill over to the left and the summit of Screel Hill can be seen ahead. Make your way through the rocks – the path becomes indistinct at this point and you have to cross some marshy ground – on to the ridge and follow it as it curves gradually to the left to reach the summit cairn Ⓑ. There are fine views from here: in one direction along the Solway coast and over the water to the line of the Cumbrian fells on the horizon; in the other direction across to the Galloway hills. Below, Castle Douglas can clearly be seen beside Carlingwark Loch.

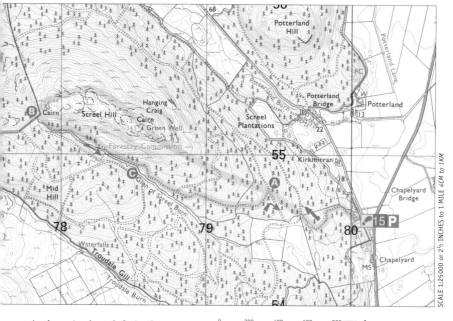

At the cairn bear left, in the direction of Bengairn, to a white-topped post and take a steeply descending, winding path.

Continue along the edge of the forest, by a wall on the right, but look out for where a waymark directs you to turn left along a path through the conifers.

Screel Hill

Head gently downhill to emerge on to a grassy track **C**.

Continue downhill and look out for where white-topped posts appear on both sides of the track **A**. Here turn right to re-enter the gloomy section of the walk and retrace your steps down to the start. ●

Mabie Forest

Start	Mabie Forest, off A710 Dumfries–New Abbey road
Distance	5½ miles (8.9km)
Approximate time	3 hours
Parking	Forestry Commission's Mabie Forest car park
Refreshments	None
Ordnance Survey maps	Landranger 84 (Dumfries & Castle Douglas), Pathfinder 529, NX87/98 (Dumfries)

If ever a forest contradicted the myth that woodland plantations are inevitably monotonous, it has to be Mabie Forest. This is a most attractive and varied walk that winds its way up and down the wooded slopes above the River Nith. The woodland is mixed with plenty of broad-leaved trees as well as conifers and all the paths and tracks are well surfaced. At regular intervals superb views open up, sometimes across the Nith estuary and Solway Firth, at other times looking inland towards Dumfries and the line of the Southern Uplands. The route is easy to follow as it is a combination of two Forestry Commission trails; simply look out for the yellow- and white-topped posts.

Start at the bottom end of the car park by the adventure playground. Follow yellow- and white-topped posts along a path into the trees, go round two bends and keep ahead – do not turn right over the footbridge – beside Mabie Burn on the right. At a T-junction turn left across a footbridge and head steadily uphill along a twisting path.

Cross a track, continue uphill and at the next track, a flat and fairly straight one, turn right. Look out for a track on the left, turn left along this track, now following white posts only, and after a few yards turn right on to a path.

Climb some steps, keep ahead and the path bends right and left to pass to the right of the small Dalshinnie Loch Ⓐ. Continue up to a track, cross over and take the path ahead, now climbing more steeply.

Go round a right-hand bend Ⓑ to continue along a pleasant section of the walk, with views of Criffel and the Solway through trees on the right. Eventually the path bends right, down to a track. Turn left along this track, here rejoining the yellow route, until the yellow and white waymarks direct you to the right on to a path. At a crossroads of paths the route continues to the left Ⓒ but keep ahead a few yards to enjoy the view.

After turning left you leave the white route and follow yellow waymarks only. Cross a track, keep ahead but on descending to a second track turn right along it Ⓓ. Just before it curves to the right, bear left on to a path, following a line of

Mabie Forest

impressive ancient beeches on the left. A brief detour to a sheltered seat on the left brings another fine viewpoint. Continue beside the beeches and head uphill, climbing steps on to a track.

Turn left and from this high-level track on the edge of the forest comes a series of grand views to the left, initially across the Nith to Dumfries

and a panorama of rolling hills beyond, later the views are across the estuary to the Solway Firth and Cumbrian mountains. Eventually, the track curves right, away from the forest edge back into the trees.

Look out for where you turn left **E** down steps, rejoining the white route, and head downhill. Cross a burn, turn left along what is now a wide track and keep another sharp look out for where you turn left off the track down to cross a footbridge over the burn. The path continues alongside the burn, descending gently and turning right to re-cross it. Keep ahead to reach an open, grassy area and walk across it, passing to the right of the site of an old, partially retained sawmill. Cross a footbridge to return to the start. ●

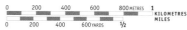

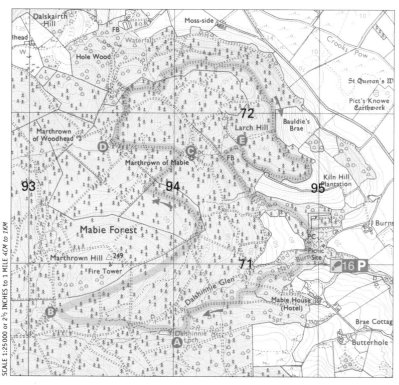

SCALE 1:25 000 or 2½ INCHES to 1 MILE 4CM to 1KM

Devil's Beef Tub

Start	Devil's Beef Tub, at Covenanters' Monument on east side of A701, about 5 miles (8km) north of Moffat
Distance	5½ miles (8.9km)
Approximate time	3 hours
Parking	Layby just to the south of Covenanters' Monument; others nearby
Refreshments	None
Ordnance Survey maps	Landranger 78 (Nithsdale & Annandale), Pathfinder 483, NT01/11 (White Coomb)

The Devil's Beef Tub, a large, deep, natural depression at the head of Annandale, acquired its name from its earlier reputation as a place where the Border reivers (gangs of marauders and thieves) used to hide their stolen cattle. It can easily be viewed from the A701 but it is seen to much greater effect on this walk which encircles three sides of it and climbs Annanhead Hill and Great Hill, both dramatic vantage points overlooking it. To complete the circuit entails a steep and difficult ascent and descent and it is better to retrace your steps from the summit of Great Hill. Expect some boggy walking in places across rough, grassy moorland.

The Covenanters' Monument

At the side of the road a gate gives access to the Covenanters' Monument and immediately provides a glorious view over the Devil's Beef Tub. The monument is one of many scattered throughout Dumfries and Galloway to the Covenanters of the 17th century, persecuted and executed for refusing to accept the king as head of the Scottish Church.

Facing the Devil's Beef Tub, turn left along the road – there

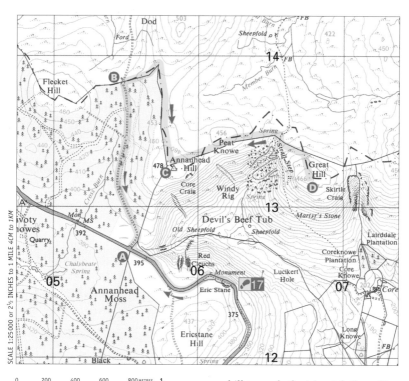

is a verge – and after ¹⁄₂ mile (800m) turn right **A** through a gate and walk along a track by the edge of Racleuch Forest. The track bears left, continues gently uphill between conifers and goes through a gate to emerge from the trees. From here there is a fine view over the rolling Tweedsmuir Hills and in the depression ahead is the source of the River Tweed. The Devil's Beef Tub itself is the source of the Annan.

Turn right **B** and keep alongside a wire fence bordering the forest on the right, heading steadily uphill across rough, tussocky grass. The moorland here is badly drained and likely to be waterlogged and muddy. Follow the fence where it turns right, initially still keeping along the forest edge, but later the fence bears slightly left away from it and continues steadily uphill towards the triangulation pillar seen ahead on the summit of Annanhead Hill (1569ft/478m). At a fence corner the route continues to the left **C** but a detour of a few yards through a gate to the triangulation pillar will reward you with a fine and extensive view over the forested slopes of the Southern Uplands.

After turning left keep alongside a wall – later a wire fence – on the right, descending into the col between Annanhead Hill and Great Hill. All the time there are superb views of the Devil's Beef Tub to the right. At the col, turn right through a gate and turn left to continue, by a wall and wire fence on the left, over Great Hill, bearing right to reach the 1531-ft (466m) summit **D**. Here are even more spectacular views over the encircling hills, with the Devil's Beef Tub immediately below.

From here retrace your steps back to the start. ●

Loch Trool

Start	Caldons Campsite, 1½ miles (2.4km) east of Glen Trool Visitor Centre at Stroan Bridge
Distance	5½ miles (8.9km)
Approximate time	3 hours
Parking	Forestry Commission car parks at Caldons Campsite. There are two car parks for day visitors either side of the bridge over Water of Trool
Refreshments	None
Ordnance Survey maps	Landranger 77 (Dalmellington to New Galloway), Pathfinder 526, NX27/37 (Glentrool Village & Bargrennan), Outdoor Leisure Map 32 (Galloway Forest Park)

This is arguably the finest short walk in Dumfries and Galloway. For a modest distance and moderate effort, you enjoy the most outstanding views across Loch Trool to the surrounding peaks from many different angles as you circuit the loch. The route is well waymarked and easy to follow but there is likely to be some muddy and rough stretches. It is worth choosing a fine day and taking your time over this walk.

The area around Loch Trool is associated with some of the most momentous events in Scottish history. A short distance (and signposted) from the start is the Martyr's Tomb, marking the place where six Covenanters were executed in 1685 for refusing to accept Charles II as head of the Church of Scotland. The route later passes the site of a battle between the Scots and English in 1307, and the Bruce Stone which commemorates Robert the Bruce's victory in that battle.

Start at the bridge over the Water of Trool and bear left, following for the first half of the walk both Southern Upland Way marker posts and green-topped 'Loch Trool Trail' posts. Turn left to cross a footbridge over Caldons Burn, continue along a

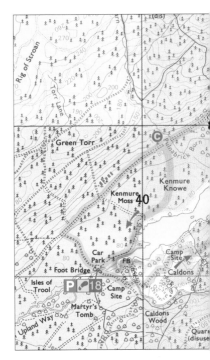

path beside it and pass the toilet block to reach a tarmac drive. Turn left through the campsite and by the shop on the right, turn left again continue along the tarmac drive which curves to the right. Turn left along a track, following the waymarks, cross a burn and shortly bear right along a path through woodland. The path curves uphill to a kissing-gate . Go through to enter conifer plantations.

The next part of the walk is particularly attractive as you follow a switchback route – with some quite steep climbs at times – through woodland above Loch Trool. The views across the water to the hills on the north side, including a striking view of Merrick at one point, are magnificent.

Near the end of the loch the path passes the location of the Battle of Glentrool in 1307 where the Scots, under Robert the Bruce, ambushed an English army and defeated it by rolling boulders down the steep slopes on to the English cavalry.

Eventually the path descends to Glenhead Burn Ⓐ. Cross the footbridge ahead, here leaving the Southern Upland Way, turn left alongside the tree-lined burn and bear right away from it, following green-topped posts, to a track. Turn left and now comes another attractive part of the walk as you proceed through delightful deciduous woodland. After crossing Gairland Burn the track ascends to a gate. Go through, keep ahead to cross a bridge over Buchan Burn and follow the track uphill. Just after a right bend, turn left along an uphill path to Bruce's Stone Ⓑ, a fine viewpoint overlooking Loch Trool and the scene of the king's victory in 1307.

Turn right to rejoin the track by a car park and turn left along a lane,

SCALE 1:25 000 or 2½ INCHES to 1 MILE 4CM to 1KM

passing through a second car park. Continue along the lane for 1 mile (1.6km) and look out for where a green-topped post directs you to turn left into conifer woodland .

Cross a footbridge over a burn and then follow a winding and undulating path back through the trees to the start.

If the last part of the walk – between point *and the start – is closed for felling operations, simply continue along the lane to the entrance to Caldons Campsite and turn left along the tarmac drive to return to the start.*

Loch Trool

St Ninian's Cave and Burrow Head

Start	Kidsdale car park. Take A746 south- west from Whithorn, turn left on to A747 and turn right along lane signposted to Kidsdale car park
Distance	7½ miles (12.1km); shorter version 2 miles (3.2km)
Approximate time	3½ hours; 1 hour for shorter walk
Parking	Kidsdale
Refreshments	None
Ordnance Survey maps	Landranger 83 (Newton Stewart & Kirkcudbright), Pathfinder 574, NX33/43 (Burrow Head & Isle of Whithorn)

A short walk through the beautiful, wooded Physgill Glen brings you to the coast by St Ninian's Cave. After visiting this historic site, associated with the beginnings of Scottish Christianity, the shorter version of the walk returns directly to the start, but the full walk heads eastwards across the cliffs to the prominent headland of Burrow Head. The coastal scenery between St Ninian's Cave and Burrow Head is superb.

Turn left out of the car park, passing to the right of the farm buildings at Kidsdale, and at a signpost to St Ninian's Cave turn right **A** along a track. This straight track – it later narrows to a path – leads through the steep-sided, wooded Physgill Glen, keeping to the right of a burn. In late spring the ground is carpeted with bluebells. After passing through a gate, the path becomes less wooded and then emerges on to a stony beach **B**.

Turn right to St Ninian's Cave **C**. St Ninian is alleged to have founded the first church in Scotland at nearby Whithorn in AD 397; the legendary *Candida Casa* or White House. In the following centuries a great monastery was established on the site and the shrine of St Ninian became a major centre of pilgrimage.

St Ninian's Cave

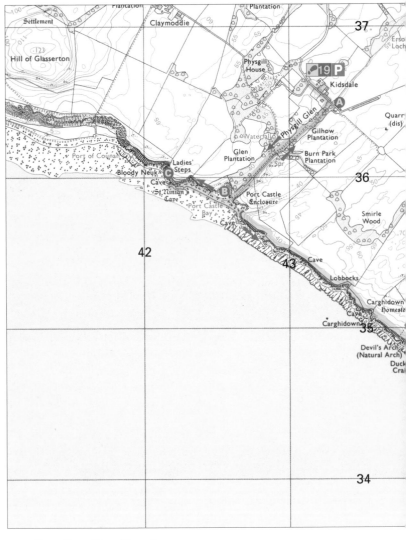

0	200 400 600	800 METRES **1**
		KILOMETRES MILES
0	200 400	600 YARDS **½**

Several Scottish kings and queens made the journey to Whithorn, the last being Mary Queen of Scots in 1567. The monastery was also the cathedral of the medieval bishops of Galloway. According to legend, St Ninian used this cave as a retreat and therefore it also attracted the attention of the pilgrims, along with the 12th-century St Ninian's Chapel a few miles away at Isle of Whithorn.

Return to the start of the path through Physgill Glen **Ⓑ**.

For the shorter walk, turn left here and retrace your steps to the car park.

For the full walk, carry on to the far end of the beach and take the path ahead that climbs steeply on to the cliff top. Now follows a fine, bracing and spectacular walk along the cliffs. At first keep by a wire fence on the right but look out for where you pass to the other side of it to climb a stile. Continue, now with the fence on the left, but take care as there are some

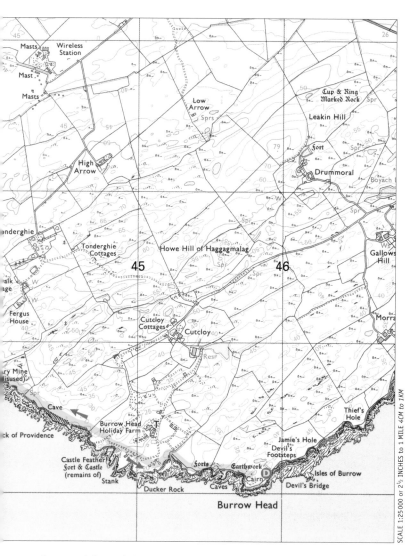

SCALE 1:25 000 or 2½ INCHES to 1 MILE 4CM to 1KM

steep drops and the path is narrow in places. After climbing a ladder-stile the route heads across more open, grassy expanses – an undulating route with a few burns to ford – to a stone stile. Climb it and continue to a gate, beyond which is a holiday park.

Go through the gate and follow the coast along the edge of the park. Exit via a stile and head up to the cairn on Burrow Head **D** where you can enjoy the grand and extensive views.

From here retrace your steps back to the start. ●

Cliffs near St Ninian's Cave

Portpatrick and Killantringan Fell

Start	Portpatrick
Distance	8 miles (12.9km)
Approximate time	4 hours
Parking	Portpatrick
Refreshments	Pubs and cafés at Portpatrick
Ordnance Survey maps	Landranger 82 (Stranraer & Glenluce), Pathfinder 537, NW95/96/97 (Portpatrick & Kirkcolm)

The starting point of the walk is also the starting point for the 212-mile (340km) Southern Upland Way. This route follows the first 4 miles (6.4km) of the Southern Upland Way and then retraces steps; a highly enjoyable walk that provides spectacular cliff scenery and fine views along the coast. There are several climbs up and down cliffs and the short ascent of Killantringan Fell is across rough ground.

Situated amidst beautiful cliff scenery and sandy beaches and with cottages grouped around a small fishing harbour, it is not surprising that Portpatrick has developed into a popular though quiet resort. But for its exposed position on the west coast of Galloway, it might have become a major port – it is the nearest point on the British mainland to Ireland – but it lost out to Stranraer at the head of the sheltered Loch Ryan. Portpatrick gets its name from St Patrick who is alleged to have crossed over from Ireland in one stride. Just behind the harbour are the ruins of a 17th-century church with a round tower.

The walk begins at the harbour. Facing the sea, turn right along the road and follow the harbour round to the left to the shelter at the base of the cliffs that marks the official start of the Southern Upland Way.

From here climb the zigzag steps on to the cliff top, pass to the left of a British Telecom Radio Station and turn right up steps to a lane Ⓐ. Turn left – there is a golf course on the right – and the lane becomes first a rough track and then narrows to a cliff-top path. Descend more zigzag steps to a bay, cross a stony beach, climb steps on the other side and turn left at a Southern Upland Way post. Shortly walk across another stony beach where there is a footbridge over a burn.

Pass through a gap in the cliffs on the right, looking out for the waymarked posts, and then ascend two series of steps. These are rough, deep and difficult in places, but there is a chain provided for support.

At the top of the steps turn left over a stile and continue along the smooth, grassy cliffs. Soon the

SCALE 1:25000 or 2½ INCHES to 1 MILE 4CM to 1KM

lighthouse on Black Head is seen ahead and you follow a well-waymarked, undulating route towards it, negotiating a kissing-gate and stile on the way.

Pass to the right of the lighthouse to reach a tarmac lane **B** and turn right along it. To the left are lovely views along the length of Killantringan Bay.

Just after the lane bends left by Killantringan Cottage, turn right **C** and head up the rough, grassy slopes (likely to be muddy and boggy near the bottom) of Killantringan Fell.

Carefully pick your way between the rocks and gorse to reach the triangulation pillar on the summit **D**. Although only 497ft (151m) high, this is a grand viewpoint, both along the coast in both directions and over inland Galloway.

Retrace your steps to the start, taking particular care on the descent of the deep steps to Maidenhead Bay. Approaching Portpatrick you enjoy superb views over the harbour. ●

Manquhill Hill

Start	Stroanpatrick, on B729, 2 miles (3.2km) north-east of junction with B7000 and ¾ mile (1.2km) east of bridge over Water of Ken
Distance	7½ miles (12.1km)
Approximate time	3½ hours
Parking	On verge in front of tin hut at Stroanpatrick
Refreshments	None
Ordnance Survey maps	Landranger 77 (Dalmellington to New Galloway), Pathfinder 504, NX69/79 (Water of Ken)

This is a walk of wide and sweeping vistas across an austere, largely empty but undeniably beautiful landscape of rolling hills, typical of the Southern Uplands. It follows a lonely stretch of the Southern Upland Way from the tiny hamlet of Stroanpatrick over the slopes of Manquhill Hill, an easy ascent. The return is an equally easy descent along a clear track. It is advisable not to attempt this walk in misty weather.

Facing the tin hut, turn right along the road and at a Southern Upland Way fingerpost turn right on to a track Ⓐ. In front of the gate to Stroanpatrick Farm, bear left to ford a burn and climb a stile. Keep ahead to a Southern Upland Way post and turn right to follow a reasonably clear path – likely to be muddy in places – keeping roughly parallel to a wall on the right.

The path climbs gently, there are several burns to ford, some stiles to climb and regular marker posts to show the way. All around are superb views: behind, the Rhinns of Kells and in front, the Carsphairn range.

After climbing a ladder-stile the wall on the right ends and the path – clearer now and better drained – continues steadily uphill across the open hillside, planted with young conifers. Later it climbs more steeply over the left shoulder of Manquhill

Hill (1382ft/421m) and then descends gently into the col between Manquhill Hill and Benbrack which looms ahead. Away to the left are extensive conifer plantations.

On meeting a broad stony track Ⓑ turn sharp right on to it. The track curves right and heads gently downhill below Manquhill Hill. At a T-junction of tracks turn left, and at the next one immediately in front turn right Ⓒ. Keep ahead to go through a metal gate, cross a bridge over a burn and continue by the burn on the right. Go through another metal gate, pass to the right of a farm (Cornharrow), climb a stile and cross a bridge over a tributary burn.

Follow the track for 1 mile (1.6km) to a road and turn right Ⓓ to return to the start. ●

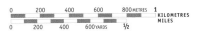

0	200	400	600	800 METRES	1
					KILOMETRES
					MILES
0	200	400	600 YARDS	½	

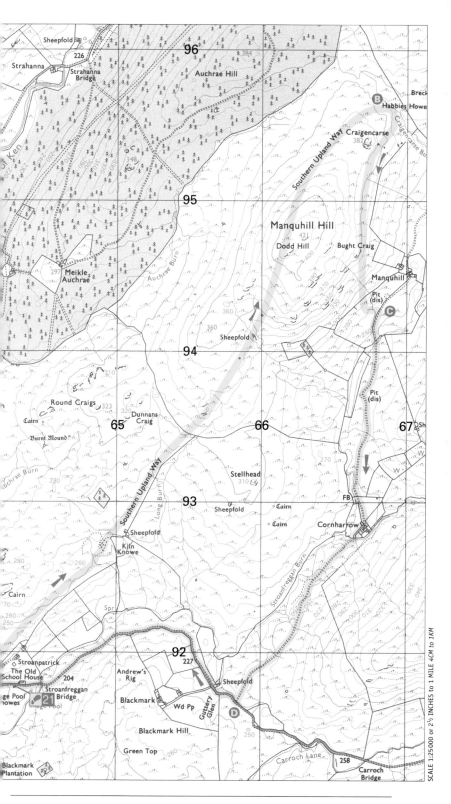

Cairnsmore of Dee

Start	Clatteringshaws Loch Wildlife Centre
Distance	6 miles (9.7km)
Approximate time	3½ hours
Parking	Clatteringshaws Loch Wildlife Centre
Refreshments	Café at Wildlife Centre
Ordnance Survey maps	Landranger 77 (Dalmellington to New Galloway), Outdoor Leisure Map 32 (Galloway Forest Park)

Cairnsmore or Black Craig of Dee is the prominent hill seen to the south of the road between New Galloway and Clatteringshaws Loch. The first part of the walk from the shores of the loch to the summit of Benniguinea is an easy and gradual climb, mostly through forest, along wide, well-surfaced tracks. The second part from Benniguinea to the 1616-ft (493m) summit of Cairnsmore of Dee crosses much rougher and more difficult terrain. There are splendid views throughout but this walk should not be undertaken in bad weather unless experienced in such conditions.

Clatteringshaws Loch Wildlife Centre is well worth a visit and, although not on our route, a path leads northwards from it to Bruce's Stone at Raploch Moss, commemorating a victory here by the Scottish king in 1307. Clatteringshaws Loch is a large reservoir created in 1931 as part of the Galloway hydro-electric scheme.

From the car park take the track on the opposite side of the road, passing

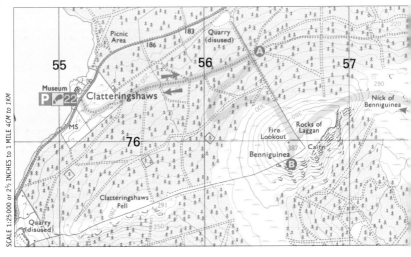

Clatteringshaws Loch

a cattle-grid, and the track winds gently up to a stile beside a gate. Climb the stile and continue steadily uphill along a straight track mostly through an area of felled forest.

At a meeting of tracks, turn sharp right Ⓐ and continue up a winding track to the cairn and prominent mast on the summit of Benniguinea (1269ft/387m). The views, especially over Clatteringshaws Loch, are well worth the climb.

Retrace your steps for a few yards to the first bend and then head straight across towards Cairnsmore of Dee.

First descend into the col between the two peaks, by a young plantation on the left, and then head steeply up the ridge to the cairn and triangulation pillar on the summit Ⓒ. The going is quite rough underfoot – no visible path, coarse and tussocky grass, rocky, heathery, and with soft ground and mud in places. However, the extensive panoramic views more than compensate for the effort.

From here retrace your steps to the start, enjoying more fine views across the loch on the descent. ●

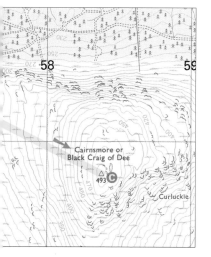

Sweetheart Abbey and Criffel

Start	New Abbey
Distance	6½ miles (10.5km)
Approximate time	4½ hours
Parking	New Abbey
Refreshments	Pubs and café at New Abbey
Ordnance Survey maps	Landranger 84 (Dumfries & Castle Douglas), Pathfinder 542, NX86/96 (Dalbeattie & New Abbey)

Rising abruptly above the western side of the Nith estuary, the conical-shaped, isolated hill of Criffel is one of the most distinctive and easily recognisable landmarks on the Solway coast. Although of relatively modest height, (1868ft/569m), the ascent from New Abbey, which starts virtually from sea level, is both lengthy and continuous and certainly gives the impression that you have climbed much higher. Not surprisingly, the views from the summit are superb, extending to the Isle of Man on clear days. Muddy conditions can be expected in places and this walk is not recommended in bad weather unless you are experienced and equipped for such conditions.

Dominating the very attractive village of New Abbey are the imposing, red sandstone ruins of Sweetheart Abbey. This 'new abbey' was founded in 1273 and gets its name because its foundress, Devorgilla, was so fond of her husband, John Balliol, that she kept his embalmed heart after his death and had it buried with her in the abbey after she died in 1290. Although few of the domestic buildings survive, the church, which dates from the 13th and 14th centuries, is almost complete apart from the roof and windows. Particularly impressive is the west front, nave and central tower.

Start in the Square and, facing the Abbey Arms, take the road to the right. At a sign 'Pedestrian Way to Waterloo Monument' turn left along a tarmac drive, by the pond of an 18th-century corn mill on the right, and follow it around a right bend. Look out for some steps on the left, climb them and walk along a narrow path between hedges.

Go through a kissing-gate , keep ahead by the left edge of a field to go through another gate and climb a stile to rejoin the tarmac drive **A**. Continue along the drive for about

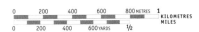

0	200	400	600	800 METRES	1	
						KILOMETRES
						MILES
0	200	400	600 YARDS	½		

Sweetheart Abbey

½ mile (800m). The Waterloo Monument, begun in 1815, the year of the battle, can be seen to the right. Where the drive ends there is a fork ahead. Take the left-hand track **B** – not the one to the monument – cross a bridge over Glen Burn and keep ahead, later continuing along a path to the right of a cottage. Climb a stile and follow the path to the left, heading gently uphill to reach a forest track **C**.

Turn right, follow the track around a left bend but at a right bend turn left off it and head across to a wire fence. Now begins the long, steady and relentless climb to the summit of Criffel. Turn right and head uphill alongside the fence – and beyond that a parallel wall – on the left. Where wall and fence diverge, keep by the wall, climb a stone stile in a wall ahead and continue up more steeply to another stile where a wire fence meets the wall. Climb it and continue along the indistinct but nevertheless visible path that bisects the wall and fence, heading steeply uphill to the cairn on the 1476-ft (450m) summit of Knockendoch **D**. The superb all-round views are simply a taste of what is to come.

Criffel is straight ahead. The path bears right and you follow it along a ridge, curving gradually left in an arc, to the triangulation pillar on the summit **E**. The views are tremendous and include the Solway coast, Cumbrian mountains, Nith estuary, Sweetheart Abbey, Loch Kindar and the line of the Southern Uplands. In very clear conditions the Isle of Arran and Isle of Man can be seen.

Retrace your steps back over Knockendoch and down to the forest track. On the descent there are more enjoyable views of Loch Kindar, Sweetheart Abbey and the Solway. Turn right along the track but instead of shortly turning left to continue on the outward route **C**, stay on it and head gently downhill to a stile. Climb it, walk through a plantation and go through a metal gate at the far end. Continue across a field, go through a metal gate and cross a footbridge over a burn **F**. The track swings right, passes through another metal gate and continues along the left inside edge of woodland.

Go through a metal gate, walk along an enclosed track, go through another gate and continue by a wall on the left, soon bending left to go through yet another metal gate. Continue along a track and bear right through white gates to reach the edge of a new housing estate.

Just before reaching a road, turn left along a track and where it bends left, turn right over a stone stile. Continue along a path through trees, by garden fences on the right, descend steps and turn right over a plank footbridge to pass in front of an old mill building. Follow a path to the left around the side of the mill and walk along the track ahead. Where the track bends right, keep ahead along a concrete path, between a wall on the left and wire fence on the right, to a road. Turn left back to New Abbey. ●

Cairnsmore of Fleet

Start	Cairnsmore Farm. From the A75 take unsigned road south-east of Palnure (just beyond bridge over Palnure Burn), keep ahead by a ruined viaduct through gates to the Cairnsmore Estate. After ½ mile (800m) pass to the left of Cairnsmore Farm, turn right around the end of the buildings and turn left at a T-junction to the parking area.
Distance	6½ miles (10.5km)
Approximate time	3½ hours
Parking	By Cairnsmore Farm
Refreshments	None
Ordnance Survey maps	Landranger 83 (Newton Stewart & Kirkcudbright), Pathfinder 540, NX46/56 (Newton Stewart)

Although Cairnsmore of Fleet is among the higher Galloway hills (2331ft/711m), the ascent of it could hardly be easier or more straightforward and on a fine day it would be an ideal introduction for anyone who has not scaled such heights before. The climb is steady, with no difficult or strenuous stretches, the path is clear throughout and the views over the Galloway hills, Cree estuary and Solway coast are magnificent.

Right from the start of the walk there is a fine view of your goal. Begin by turning left out of the parking area along a track to a metal gate. Go through the gate and bear right diagonally uphill across a field – later passing between gorse bushes – to go through another metal gate in the top corner **A**. Follow the path ahead through conifers, climb a stile and

Cairnsmore of Fleet

Memorial on summit of Cairnsmore of Fleet

continue steadily uphill. Pass through a wall gap, cross a track and eventually emerge from the trees to reach a ladder-stile. Ahead the path can be clearly seen, ascending the grassy and heathery slopes of Cairnsmore of Fleet.

Climb the ladder-stile, pass through another wall gap **Ⓑ** and the path now winds uphill more steeply. Near the top it flattens out and follows a line of cairns to the memorial stone, erected to the memory of all airmen killed in aircraft crashes on the mountain in World War II.

Just beyond is the summit cairn and triangulation pillar **Ⓒ** from where there are magnificent views over the Galloway hills (including Merrick), Cree estuary, Wigtown and Luce Bays, the Machars, Mull of Galloway and, in clear conditions, the Isle of Man, Cumbrian fells and Northern Ireland.

Retrace your steps downhill to the start, enjoying more splendid views across the Cree estuary below. ●

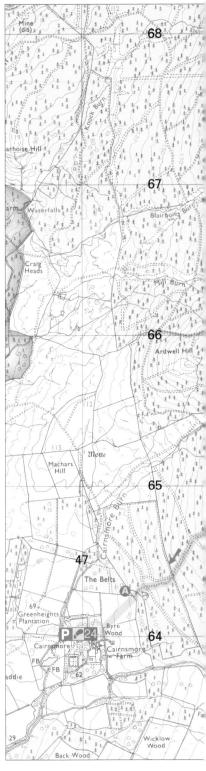

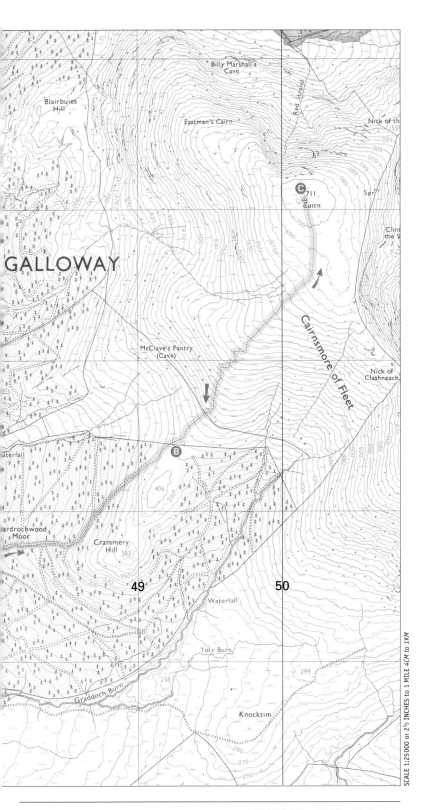

GALLOWAY

SCALE 1:25000 or 2½ INCHES to 1 MILE 4CM to 1KM

Black Hill and Well Hill

Start	Durisdeer
Distance	5½ miles (8.9km)
Approximate time	3½ hours
Parking	By the church and war memorial at Durisdeer
Refreshments	None
Ordnance Survey maps	Landranger 78 (Nithsdale & Annandale), Pathfinder 494, NS80/90 (Mennock & Durisdeer)

Despite a relatively modest height of 1744ft (531m), the initial climb to the summit of Black Hill is hard work: steep, long – 1¼ miles (2km) – pathless and over rough terrain. Once the triangulation pillar is reached, the going becomes easier as you descend into a col and then steadily climb again to the higher summit of Well Hill (1987ft/606m). Then comes a very steep descent to a track, followed by a relaxing finale as you gently descend along this track, the Well Path, an ancient routeway that dates back to Roman times. The views over Nithsdale and the Lowther Hills from the higher points are magnificent. As you are dependent on certain landmarks, this walk should on no account be attempted in bad weather, especially misty conditions.

It is surprising to find such a large and elegant church in a village as small as Durisdeer. The reason is that it was built by the first Duke of Queensberry of nearby Drumlanrig Castle and the north wing was the Queensberry mausoleum. The church dates from 1699 and retains the old box pews.

Begin by taking the lane to the right of Durisdeer church. After passing between cottages and going through a metal gate, the lane becomes a rough track. This is the Well Path, an ancient route through the hills. Of Roman origin, it was later used by medieval pilgrims, including several Scottish kings, on their way to the shrine of St Ninian at Whithorn.

You soon leave the Well Path by turning left through the first metal gate **A** and descending steeply to ford Kirk Burn. This might be difficult after wet weather. Head up the other side, pass through a wall gap and climb steeply over the hill ahead. To the right are fine views up the valley of Kirk Burn and behind, Durisdeer church can be seen half-hidden by a circle of trees, with Nithsdale in the distance. At the top descend into a col to reach a gate in a wire fence just to the left of a circular enclosure. Go through and now climb more steeply across rough grass and heather up the flanks of Black Hill. After the final steep pull up to the summit plateau, head across to the triangulation pillar **B**. The magnificent panoramic views

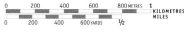

SCALE 1:25000 or 2½ INCHES to 1 MILE 4CM to 1KM

include Criffel on the Solway coast, the main Galloway range, the Lowther Hills and the Border hills.

At the triangulation pillar turn right and descend across rough grass, later making for and keeping by a wire fence on the left. In the col between Black Hill and Well Hill turn left through a gate and turn right to continue uphill again, now with a wire fence on the right. Keep by this fence – there is later a parallel wall as well – around right and left bends, climbing to the summit of Well Hill **C**, another superb viewpoint.

At the summit turn right through a gate and descend steeply, keeping beside a wire fence and wall on the right, to a track. Turn right  D, go through a gate and follow this track gently downhill through a pass in the hills to return to the start. The actual Well Path runs parallel just below in the valley on the right and as you descend, the outline of a Roman fort can be seen beside it. A little further on the Well Path joins the track and you keep along it for the last $\frac{1}{2}$ mile (800m) into Durisdeer.

Durisdeer church

Caldons Burn and Lamachan Hill

Start	Caldons Campsite, 1½ miles (2.4km) east of Glen Trool Visitor Centre at Stroan Bridge
Distance	8½ miles (13.7km)
Approximate time	5½ hours
Parking	Forestry Commission car parks at Caldons Campsite. There are two car parks for day visitors either side of the bridge over Water of Trool
Refreshments	None
Ordnance Survey maps	Landranger 77 (Dalmellington to New Galloway), Pathfinder 526, NX27/37 (Glentrool Village & Bargrennan), Outdoor Leisure Map 32 (Galloway Forest Park)

Lamachan Hill is the highest peak in the Minnigaff range that lies to the south of Loch Trool and is flanked by Larg Hill to the west and Bennanbrack to the east. A delightful, though rocky and sometimes muddy walk beside Caldons Burn through the forest leads on to the open hillside for a steady climb to the 2350-ft (717m) summit. From here there are stunning views. The return descends to the col between Lamachan Hill and Larg Hill, and continues over the top of Craignaw to re-enter the forest and rejoin Caldons Burn. This walk should not be attempted in bad, especially misty, weather, unless experienced in such conditions and able to navigate by using a compass.

Start at the bridge over the Water of Trool and bear left alongside the river, temporarily joining the Southern Upland Way. Do not cross the next bridge but bear right to keep by the right bank of Caldons Burn, passing through the campsite and across a play area.

Continue along a winding path through trees. This is a most attractive path but the going can be difficult, with wet, muddy and rocky sections and overhanging branches at times. The route keeps by or above the burn, climbing all the while, negotiating a stile, crossing a track, passing waterfalls and at one stage going through a virtual ravine. Continue along the right bank of Caldons Burn to where you ford Mulmein Burn, a tributary burn Ⓐ.

Now cross a wall on the left and continue by the wall on the right. Cross a wire fence, turn left to ford Caldons Burn, cross another wall and turn right to continue uphill, by a wall on the right. Soon you emerge from the forest and head more steeply uphill, between Cambrick Hill to the left and Craignaw to the right. Ford a burn and continue climbing, keeping by the wall on the right all the while, to the summit cairn on Lamachan Hill Ⓑ. From here there are splendid all-round views over the Galloway hills.

At the cairn turn right and follow a line of iron fence posts gently downhill into the col between Lamachan Hill and Larg Hill which lies ahead Ⓒ. Turn right and continue downhill, initially by a wall on the left but later bearing away from the wall in the direction of the prominent bulk of Craignaw, seen on the ascent. Descend into a dip and

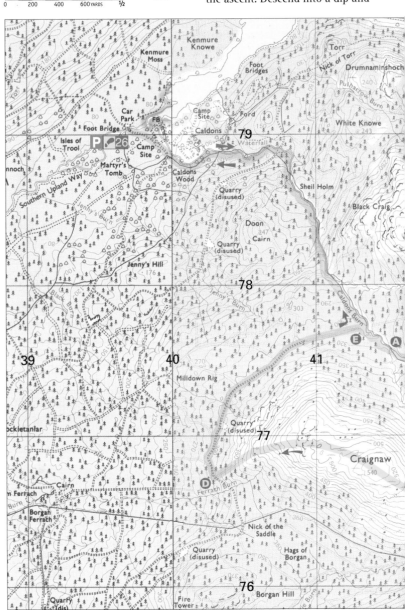

View from the summit of Craignaw

then climb quite steeply to the summit cairn (1772ft/540m). Behind is a striking view of the Larg Hill-Lamachan Hill-Bennanbrack ridge.

Continue along the ridge – there are a number of 'ups and downs' – over rough, tussocky grass and bear left towards the edge of the conifers below. On this part of the walk you may be lucky enough to see some wild goats. Turn left at the corner of the forest and follow a grassy ride steeply downhill to a track **D**. Turn right along it, passing a disused quarry, and the track bears right. Where it ends, keep ahead along another grassy ride between conifers, to emerge on to the path above Caldons Burn **E**.

Turn left and retrace your steps downhill beside the burn to the starting point. ●

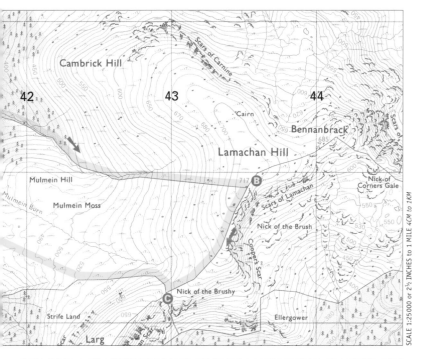

SCALE 1:25000 or 2½ INCHES to 1 MILE 4CM to 1KM

Colvend Coast

Colvend Coast

Start	Kippford
Distance	10 miles (16.1km)
Approximate time	5 hours
Parking	Kippford
Refreshments	Pubs at Kippford, café at Colvend
Ordnance Survey maps	Landranger 84 (Dumfries & Castle Douglas), Pathfinder 555, NX85/95 (Dalbeattie Forest)

Colvend refers to the stretch of the Solway coast between Rough Firth and Sandyhills Bay. It is an outstandingly attractive and spectacular coastline but the inland part of the walk, mainly through forest, is scarcely any less enjoyable and there is a succession of splendid views throughout. This is a lengthy and quite energetic walk, particularly the section along the coast path, but a highly memorable one, especially on a fine and clear day, and well worth taking plenty of time over.

In the 19th century, Kippford had a busy ship repair and building yard but the River Urr silted up and now it has become a popular boating centre and small resort.

Turn left out of the car park and walk down the road alongside the Urr estuary. At the post office turn left (No Through Road sign) up a narrow lane **A**, signposted Jubilee Path, which bends to the right and then heads uphill.

After passing the last of the houses, continue along a rocky path – there is a National Trust for Scotland sign 'Jubilee Path to Rockcliffe' – between gorse and trees. At a meeting of paths and tracks, keep ahead along a straight, wooded, enclosed track which later becomes a tarmac track. Follow the track around a sharp right bend down into the quiet coastal village of Rockcliffe and turn left alongside the beach **B**.

At a footpath sign 'To Castle Point' turn right **C** along a tarmac drive. To the right are attractive views of Rockcliffe, Rough Firth and the River Urr, with hills framing the background. At a National Trust for Scotland sign 'Footpath to Castle Point and Sandyhills', turn right on to a path that winds alternately between bushes and along the rocky shore to reach Nelson's Grave. This is nothing to do with Admiral Lord Nelson but the grave of Joseph Nelson of Whitehaven who was drowned at sea in 1791. Just after passing the grave climb a stone stile, continue along the coast path to a kissing-gate, go through and climb up to the magnificent viewpoint of Castlehill **D**, site of an ancient fort dating from around 400 BC. A toposcope enables you to identify the range of places that can be seen from here on a clear day.

Descend to go through another kissing-gate. Now follows a superb stretch of coastal walking; the path hugs the coast and keeps along the cliffs all the way, there are regular 'Coastal Path' signs and a number of stiles. This is quite an energetic part of the walk with several steep climbs and descents but the scenery is outstanding. Eventually, the path drops down to the handful of charming cottages at Port O'Warren Bay, descending a flight of steps to a stone stile.

Climb the stile and turn left uphill **E**, in the Portling, Douglas Hall and Sandyhills direction. Later, the track becomes a lane which descends to the whitewashed hamlet of Portling. Ignore a footpath sign to the right and keep ahead along the lane to a road **F**. Turn left – take care as this road can be busy – for ¾ mile (1.2km) into Colvend.

Just before reaching the garage, shop and café, turn right **G** along a track that passes to the right of the village hall. The track passes houses and heads gently uphill to enter woodland. Continue through the trees to pass by Barean Loch and keep ahead, bearing slightly left on joining another track. At a footpath sign to the A710 a few yards before reaching a fork, turn left **H** on to a path by a burn on the left. Go through a gate, walk along the left edge of rough pasture, by a wire fence and later wall on the left, and in the field corner go through another gate to the right of a cottage. Keep ahead to a tarmac track and turn right along this track as it winds steadily uphill to the A710.

Turn left and then immediately right **J** on to a track and pass beside

The Solway coast at Rockcliffe

a gate, at a 'Forest Enterprise, Mark Hill' sign. Continue along this very pleasant track, entering woodland, and from now on follow regular footpath signs to Kippford.

At a fork take the right-hand track, head up to a T-junction and turn right. The track climbs steadily and at the top grand views open up across Rough Firth and the Urr estuary to the Galloway hills.

Continue downhill to a crossroads, keep ahead and look out for a Kippford sign which directs you to the right on to a narrow path. The path winds downhill through trees and around several sharp bends to emerge on to a track. Continue down into Kippford and at the bottom turn right along the road to return to the car park.

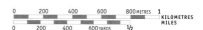

SCALE 1:25000 or 2½ INCHES to 1 MILE 4CM to 1KM

Merrick

Start	Bruce's Stone, at end of minor road on north side of Loch Trool
Distance	9½ miles (15.3km)
Approximate time	6½ hours
Parking	Bruce's Stone
Refreshments	None
Ordnance Survey maps	Landranger 77 (Dalmellington to New Galloway), Outdoor Leisure Map 32 (Galloway Forest Park)

At 2766ft (843m), the summit of Merrick is the highest point in southern Scotland. The ascent is a strenuous and challenging one and its difficulties should not be under-estimated. Allow plenty of time for the walk and it should only be attempted by reasonably fit and experienced walkers. The path by Gairland Burn – rocky and difficult in places and often muddy and waterlogged – leads past a succession of lochs to reach the shores of Loch Enoch. From here comes a very steep climb of almost 1 mile (1.6km) to the summit, from where you enjoy the most magnificent views. The descent is much easier along a well-marked path all the way. A possible alternative for less experienced walkers is to do a 'there and back' walk using the clear and well-used return route in reverse to reach the summit. It must be emphasised that this walk up Merrick should definitely not be embarked upon in poor weather conditions, especially during the winter months.

Bruce's Stone, a magnificent viewpoint overlooking Loch Trool, was erected to commemorate a victory by Robert the Bruce over the English in 1307.

Facing the stone and loch, turn left along a track, ignoring the footpath sign to Merrick unless doing the 'there and back' alternative route. The track bends right, heads downhill and bends left to cross a bridge over Buchan Burn. Keep past the first stile on the left, go through a gate and climb the next stile Ⓐ, signposted to Gairland Burn and Loch Valley. Head uphill, go through a gate, continue initially by a wall on the left and go through another gate. Now keep by the wall on the right and the path soon bears left across the bouldery slopes of Buchan Hill above Gairland Burn. Later, it descends to keep beside the burn – a lovely stretch of the walk – to reach Loch Valley. Walk along the left shore of the loch and continue beside the burn again to the beautiful, rugged and lonely shores of Loch Neldricken.

Keep along the left bank – the path becomes indistinct here – passing the infamous 'Murder Hole', a small bay at the far-western corner featured in S.R. Crockett's novel *The Raiders*. Apparently, the water never freezes over here. Bear right at the corner of the loch and head up to pass through a wall gap. Continue uphill, by a burn on the right, passing to the left of the crags of Ewe Rig. Over to the right the small Loch Arron is seen and the route continues through a pass at Craig Neldricken to descend to the shores of the wild, beautiful and island-studded Loch Enoch . Merrick rears up to the left, a daunting sight.

Turn left beside the loch, pass over a low wall and wire fence in the south-west corner and now head up the grassy slopes to the summit of Merrick. The ascent is steep and tiring but the terrain is not difficult. After

Loch Neldricken

the final steep pull up to the plateau, it is with relief and a great feeling of satisfaction that you head across to the summit cairn and triangulation pillar **C**. The outstanding panoramic views across mountains and lochs and across to Ailsa Craig on the Ayrshire coast extend, in clear weather, to the Isle of Man, Lakeland fells and the Antrim coast of Northern Ireland.

At the summit turn left and head steadily downhill, in a south-westerly direction, across the smooth, grassy plateau, following a series of cairns, towards the clear ridge ahead, called the Neive of the Spit. Later, you join and keep by a wall on the right to head gently uphill along the ridge over the summit of Benyellary (2362ft/720m) **D**.

Continue past the summit cairn, descending more steeply and still with the wall on the right. In front, the views looking towards Glen Trool are superb.

The path later veers left away from the wall down to a kissing-gate. Go through, head down to the edge of the forest and continue quite steeply downhill between conifers to a track. Turn right, cross a bridge over Whiteland Burn and immediately turn left **E**, at a footpath sign to Loch Trool, to continue downhill. The path bears right and winds through the trees, emerging from the forest at a kissing-gate.

Go through the gate and keep ahead above Buchan Burn for a most attractive finale with grand views ahead over Loch Trool to the forested slopes beyond. Go through another kissing-gate and the path leads down to the start. ●

0	200	400	600	800 METRES	1
					KILOMETRES
					MILES
0	200	400	600 YARDS	½	

SCALE 1:25000 or 2½ INCHES to 1 MILE 4CM to 1KM

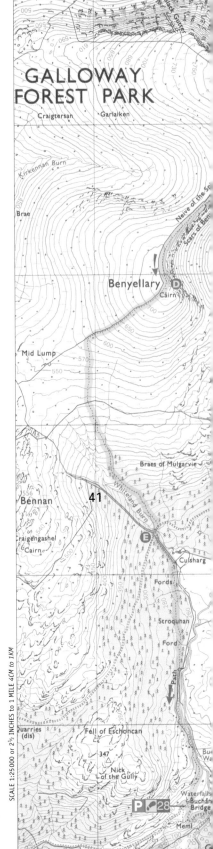

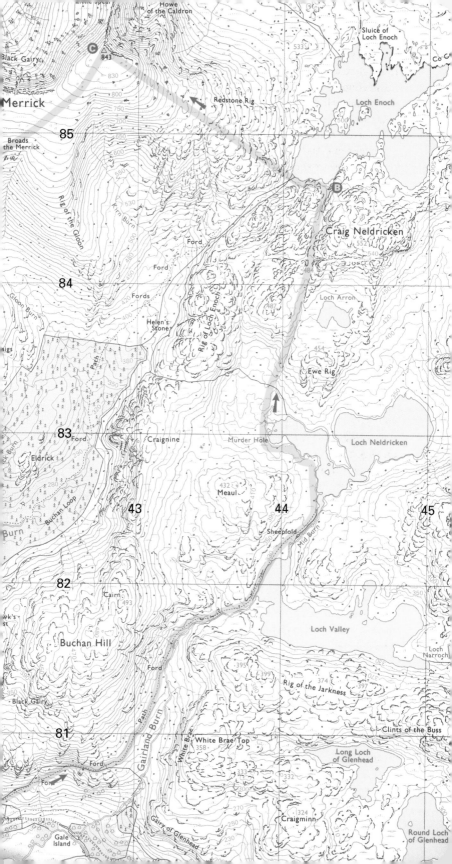

Further Information

The Law and Tradition as they affect Walking in Scotland

Walkers following the routes given in this book should not run into problems, but it is as well to know something about the law as it affects access, and also something of the traditions which can sometimes be quite different in Scotland from elsewhere in Britain. Most of this is common sense, observing the country code and having consideration for other people and their activities which, after all, may be their livelihood.

It is often said that there is no law of trespass in Scotland. In fact there is, but the trespass itself is not usually a criminal offence. You can be asked to leave any property, and technically 'reasonable force' may be used to obtain your compliance – though the term is not defined! You can be charged with causing damage due to the trespass, but this would be hard to establish if you were just walking on open, wild, hilly country where, whatever the law, in practice there has been a long tradition of free access for recreational walking – something both the Scottish Landowners' Federation and the Mountaineering Council of Scotland do not want to see changed.

There are certain restrictions. Walkers should obey the country code and seasonal restrictions arising from lambing or stalking. Where there is any likelihood of such restrictions this is mentioned in the text and visitors are asked to comply. When camping, use a campsite. Camp fires should not be lit; they are a danger to moorland and forest, and really not necessary as lightweight and efficient stoves are now available.

Many of the walks in this book are on rights of way. The watchdog on rights of way in Scotland is the Scottish Rights of Way Society (SRWS), who maintain details on all established cases and will, if need be, contest attempted closures. They produce a booklet on the Scottish legal position (*Rights of Way, A Guide to the Law in Scotland*), and their green signposts are a familiar sight by many footpaths and tracks, indicating the lines of historic routes.

In Scotland rights of way are not marked on Ordnance Survey maps as is the case south of the border. It was not felt necessary to show these as such on the maps – a further reflection of the freedom to roam that is enjoyed in Scotland. So a path on a map is no indication of a right of way, and many paths and tracks of great use to walkers were built by estates as stalking paths or for private access. While you may traverse such paths, taking due care to avoid damage to property and the natural environment, you should obey restricted access notices and leave if asked to do so.

The only established rights of way are those where a court case has resulted in a legal judgment, but there are thousands of other 'claimed' rights of way. Local planning authorities have a duty to protect rights of way – this is no easy task with only limited resources. Many attempts at closing claimed rights of way have been successfully contested in the courts by the Scottish Rights of Way Society and local authorities.

A dog on a lead or under control may also be taken on a right of way. There is little chance of meeting a free-range solitary bull on any of the walks. Any herds seen are not likely to be dairy cattle, but all cows can be inquisitive and may approach walkers, especially if they have a dog. Dogs running around among stock may be shot on the spot; this is not draconian legislation but a desperate attempt to stop sheep and lambs being harmed, driven to panic or lost, sometimes with fatal results. Any practical points or restrictions applicable will be made in the text of each walk. If there is no comment it can be assumed that the route carries no real restrictions.

Scotland in fact likes to keep everything as natural as possible, so, for instance, waymarking is kept to a minimum (the Scottish Rights of Way Society signposts and Forest Walk markers are in unobtrusive colours). In Scotland people are asked to 'walk softly in the wilderness, to take nothing except photographs, and leave nothing except footprints' – which is better than any law.

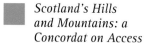

Scotland's Hills and Mountains: a Concordat on Access

This remarkable agreement was published early in 1996 and is likely to have considerable influence on walkers' rights in Scotland in the future. The signatories include organisations which have formerly been at odds - the Scottish Landowners' Federation and the Ramblers' Association, for example. However, they joined with others to make the Access Forum (a full list of signatories is detailed below). The RSPB and the National Trust for Scotland did not sign the Concordat initially but it is hoped that they will support its principles.

The organisations that have signed the Concordat are:

Association of Deer Management Groups
Convention of Scottish Local Authorities
Mountaineering Council of Scotland
National Farmers' Union of Scotland
Ramblers' Association Scotland
Scottish Countryside Activities Council
Scottish Landowners' Federation
Scottish Natural Heritage
Scottish Sports Association
Scottish Sports Council

Further Information

Bruce's Stone, Loch Trool

They agreed that the basis of access to the hills for the purposes of informal recreation should be:

Freedom of access exercised with responsibility and subject to reasonable constraints for management and conservation purposes.

Acceptance by visitors of the needs of land management, and understanding of how this sustains the livelihood, culture and community interests of those who live and work in the hills.

Acceptance by land managers of the

 ### Glossary of Gaelic Names

Many of the place-names in Scotland are Gaelic in origin, and this list gives some of the more common elements, which will allow readers to understand otherwise meaningless words and appreciate the relationship between place-names and landscape features. Place-names often have variant spellings, and the more common of these are given here.

aber	mouth of loch, river	eilidh	hind
abhainn	river	eòin, eun	bird
allt	stream	fionn	white
auch, ach	field	fraoch	heather
bal, bail, baile	town, homestead	gabhar, ghabhar,	
bàn	white, fair, pale	gobhar	goat
bealach	hill pass	garbh	rough
beg, beag	small	geal	white
ben, beinn	hill	ghlas, glas	grey
bhuidhe	yellow	gleann, glen	narrow, valley
blar	plain	gorm	blue, green
brae, braigh	upper slope, steepening	inbhir, inver	confluence
		inch, inis, innis	island, meadow by river
breac	speckled	lag, laggan	hollow
cairn	pile of stones, often marking a summit	làrach	old site
cam	crooked	làirig	pass
càrn	cairn, cairn-shaped hill	leac	slab
		liath	grey
caol, kyle	strait	loch	lake
ceann, ken, kin	head	lochan	small loch
cil, kil	church, cell	màm	pass, rise
clach	stone	maol	bald-shaped top
clachan	small village	monadh	upland, moor
cnoc	hill, knoll, knock	mór, mor(e)	big
coille, killie	wood	odhar, odhair	dun-coloured
corrie, coire, choire	mountain hollow	rhu, rubha	point
		ruadh	red, brown
craig, creag	cliff, crag	sgòr, sgòrr, sgùrr	pointed
crannog, crannag	man-made island	sron	nose
dàl, dail	field, flat	stob	pointed
damh	stag	strath	valley (broader than glen)
dearg	red		
druim, drum	long ridge	tarsuinn	traverse, across
dubh, dhu	black, dark	tom	hillock (rounded)
dùn	hill fort	tòrr	hillock (more rugged)
eas	waterfall	tulloch, tulach	knoll
eilean	island	uisge	water, river

public's expectation of having access to the hills.

Acknowledgment of a common interest in the natural beauty and special qualities of Scotland's hills, and the need to work together for their protection and enhancement.

The Forum point out that the success of the Concordat will depend on all who manage or visit the hills acting on these four principles. In addition, the parties to the Concordat will promote good practice in the form of:

- Courtesy and consideration at a personal level.

- A welcome to visitors.

- Making advice readily available on the ground or in advance.

- Better information about the uplands and hill land uses through education.

- Respect by visitors for the welfare needs of livestock and wildlife.

- Adherence to relevant codes and standards of good practice by visitors and land managers alike.

Any local restrictions on access should be essential for the needs of management, should be fully explained, and be for the minimum period and area required.

Queries should be addressed to: Access Forum Secretariat, c/o Recreation and Access Branch, Scottish Natural Heritage, 2 Anderson Place, Edinburgh EH6 5NP.

 ## Safety on the Hills

The hills, mountains and moorlands of Britain, though of modest height compared with those in many other countries, need to be treated with respect. Friendly and inviting in good weather, they can quickly be transformed into wet, misty, windswept and potentially dangerous areas of wilderness in bad weather. Even on an outwardly fine and settled summer day, conditions can rapidly deteriorate at high altitudes and, in winter, even more so.

Therefore it is advisable always to take both warm and waterproof clothing, sufficient nourishing food, a hot drink, first-aid kit, torch and whistle. Wear suitable footwear, ie. strong walking boots or shoes that give a good grip over rocky terrain and on slippery slopes. Try to obtain a local weather forecast and bear it in mind before you start. Do not be afraid to abandon your proposed route and return to your starting point in the event of a sudden and unexpected deterioration in the weather. Do not go alone and allow enough time to finish the walk well before nightfall.

Most of the walks described in this book do not venture into remote wilderness areas and will be safe to do, given due care and respect, at any time of year in all but the most unreasonable weather. Indeed, a crisp, fine winter day often provides perfect walking conditions, with firm ground underfoot and a clarity that is not possible to achieve in the other seasons of the year. A few walks, however, are suitable only for reasonably fit and experienced walkers and should definitely not be tackled during the winter months or in bad weather, especially high winds and mist. These are indicated in the general description that precedes each of the walks.

Mountain Rescue

In case of emergency the standard procedure is to dial 999 and ask for the police who will assess and deal with the situation.

First, however, render first aid as required and make sure that the casualty is made warm and comfortable. The distress signal (six flashes/whistle-blasts, repeated at intervals of one minute) may bring help from other walkers in the area. Write down essential details: exact location (six-figure grid reference), time of accident, numbers involved, details of any injuries sustained, steps already taken; then despatch a messenger to phone the police.

If leaving the casualty alone, mark the site with an eye-catching object. Be patient; waiting for help can seem interminable.

Useful Organisations

Association for the Protection of Rural Scotland
Gladstone's Land, 483 Lawnmarket, Edinburgh EH1 2NT
Tel. 0131 225 7012

Dumfries and Galloway Council
Council Offices, English Street, Dumfries DG1 2DD
Tel. 01387 260184

Forestry Commission
Information Branch, 231 Corstorphine Road, Edinburgh EH12 7AT
Tel. 0131 334 0303

Historic Scotland
Long House, Salisbury Place, Edinburgh EH9 1SH
Tel. 0131 668 8600

Long Distance Walkers' Association
c/o Les Maple, 21 Upcroft, Windsor, Berks SL4 3NH
Tel. 01753 866685

National Trust for Scotland
5 Charlotte Square, Edinburgh EH2 4DU
Tel. 0131 226 5922

Ordnance Survey
Romsey Road, Maybush, Southampton SO16 4GU
Tel. 0345 330011

Ramblers' Association (Scotland)
Crusader House, Haig Business Park, Markinch, Fife KY7 6AQ
Tel. 01592 611177

Scottish Natural Heritage
12 Hope Terrace, Edinburgh EH9 2AS
Tel. 0131 447 4784

Scottish Rights of Way Society Ltd
Unit 2, John Cotton Business Centre, 10/2 Sunnyside, Edinburgh EH7 5RA
Tel. 0131 652 2937

Scottish Wildlife Trust
Cramond House, Kirk Cramond, Cramond Glebe Road, Edinburgh EH4 6NS
Tel. 0131 312 7765

Scottish Youth Hostels Association
7 Glebe Crescent, Stirling FK8 2JA
Tel. 01786 451181

Tourist Information Centres
Dumfries and Galloway Tourist Board
Campbell House, Bankend Road, Dumfries DG1 4TH
Tel. 01387 250434

Local tourist information numbers:
Biggar: 01899 21066
Castle Douglas: 01556 502611
Dalbeattie: 01556 610117
Dumfries: 01387 253862
Gatehouse of Fleet: 01557 814212
Gretna Gateway to Scotland: 01461 338500
Gretna Green: 01461 337834
Kirkcudbright: 01557 330494
Langholm: 01387 380976
Moffat: 01683 220620
Newton Stewart: 01671 402431
Sanquhar: 01659 50185

Weather forecasts
For Scotland, 48-hour forecast. Tel. 0891 112260
UK seven-day forecast. Tel. 0891 333123

Ordnance Survey Maps of Dumfries and Galloway

Dumfries and Galloway is covered by Ordnance Survey 1:50 000 scale ($1\frac{1}{4}$ inches to 1 mile or 2cm to 1km) Landranger map sheets 76, 77, 78, 79, 82, 83, 84 and 85. These all-purpose maps are packed with information to help you explore the area and show viewpoints, picnic sites, places of interest and caravan and camping sites.

To examine the Dumfries and Galloway area in more detail, Ordnance Survey Outdoor Leisure map 32 (Galloway Forest Park) at 1:25 000 scale (2½ inches to 1 mile or 4cm to 1km) is ideal.

The following Pathfinder maps, also at 1:25 000 scale, cover the area:

481 (NS61/71)
482 (NS81/91)
483 (NT01/11)
492 (NS40/50)
493 (NS60/70)
494 (NS80/90)
495 (NT00/10)
496 (NT20/30)
504 (NX69/79)
505 (NX89/99)
506 (NY09/19)
507 (NY29/39)
508 (NY49/59)
516 (NX68/78)
517 (NX88/98)
518 (NY08/18)
519 (NY28/38)
520 (NY48/58)
525 (NX07/17)
526 (NX27/37)
528 (NX67/77)
529 (NX87/97)

530 (NY07/17)
531 (NY27/37)
532 (NY47/57)
537 (NW95/96/97)
538 (NX06/16)
539 (NX26/36)
540 (NX 46/56)
541 (NX66/76)
542 (NX86/96)
543 (NY06/16)
544 (NY26/36)
551 (NX05/15)
552 (NX25/35)
553 (NX45/55)
554 (NX65/75)
555 (NX85/95)
563 (NX03/04
& 13/14)
564 (NX34/44)
565 (NX64/74)
574 (NX33/43)

To get to Dumfries and Galloway use the Ordnance Survey Great Britain Routeplanner (Travelmaster map 1) at 1:625 000 scale (1 inch to 10 miles or 1cm to 6.25km), or Travelmaster map 4 (Southern Scotland and Northumberland) at 1:250 000 scale (1 inch to 4 miles or 1cm to 2.5km).

Ordnance Survey maps and guides are available from most booksellers, stationers and newsagents.

Merrick from Loch Enoch

Further Information

Index

Entries in italics refer to illustrations